*Dorothy, Kathie and I had a
wonderful tr.
your hospita
look forware*

Joh

Back to the Cottage

*Leadership Wisdom
for Today*

John L. Sipple

xulon PRESS

Back to the Cottage
Leadership Widom for Today
by John Sipple

Printed in the United States of America

ISBN 9781619961999

www.xulonpress.com

Table of Contents

Endorsements

L ife is a series of stories woven into a pattern that shapes and defines us. From the crucible of a small family business to leadership in a huge corporation, John Sipple learned to lead and establish values that made his leadership both different and effective. Back to the Cottage is a book on real leadership in practice, not just theory. It is values – and God based, not just a recipe for what works. John uniquely extracts principles of leadership both from his story and from the stories of others in a way that engages both your heart and your mind. This is not just leadership for industry, but leadership in all aspects of life.

Jerry White, PhD, Major General, USAF, Ret
International President Emeritus, The Navigators
Author of *Honesty, Morality and Conscience and Rules to Live By*

True leaders are those who "walk the talk". John Sipple is one of those leaders. I've known John for many years both professionally and personally. His book is a fascinating story of an individual, who from simple beginnings learned his lessons well and has continued to successfully apply these life principles throughout the unfolding tapestry of his life. As a mutual manager and consultant, I could readily identify with this book; in fact I was fortunate enough to live part of the story with John. I've always found him to be a man of character and the utmost in integrity. There are valuable lessons for all of us in this book, the sections on leadership are time-less and second to none. Good reading!

David W. Miller: President: Miller and Associates, Management Consultants

With a passion and authenticity that comes from experience and a great faith, John Sipple calls us back to a simpler view of life and business in Back to the Cottage. Drawing from his first encounter with commercial enterprise as a young boy, his success in a Fortune 500 company and his international influence as a business coach, John reveals that the keys to success of enterprise are found in the heart of the family business. Back to the Cottage mixes sound principles with engaging examples of how these principles work in any situation. Thanks John for showing us the way back to the future!

Bruce Hebel, President, Regenerating Life Ministries
Author of Forgiving Forward: Unleashing the Forgiveness Revolution

There are myriads of management and leadership books written that extol a new, undiscovered way to 'magically' make everyone a super leader. Unfortunately, the 'magic' fades quickly when it is not rooted in principles and values that have stood the test of time. In Back to the Cottage, John Sipple uses his personal journey from growing up in a family-run business to being an executive with a large corporation to discover and share those time tested principles that help make one a success in life as well as business. Back to the Cottage is an entertaining and informative read.

Robert Cary, Leadership and Organizational Consultant

Back to the Cottage is a timely reminder for many and a new concept for others, that age old principles and values, practically applied, can positively transform businesses, organizations, communities and individuals!

Rick Guthrie: Manager, Human Relations, Kearfott Corporation

Back to the Cottage is one of those books that is called 'written in due time'. Everyone in the marketplace should read this book containing transforming truths and concepts, which when implemented will give enduring and profitable results. John has in his personal DNA a business legacy that came from his grandfather and father. The wisdom nuggets throughout this book are transferrable to every business or enterprise from Mom & Pop to corporations. We highly endorse the man and his book.

  Aaron Evans, President, Emerging Daniel Company
  Author of *Emerging Daniel Company*

Real leadership seems rare in our current society. John does an excellent job describing the key aspects of leadership necessary for government, business, or charitable organizations to remain relevant in today's fast changing world.

  Dave Fraser: Comptroller, Buckeye Florida

Dedication

꩜ ꩜

To Kathie
My wife, partner and best friend.
You connected me to all that is important in life:
Jesus Christ, family, friends

To Kim and James, Kerri and Jeff, Heather and Randy,
The inspiration for this book
originated with the birth of your children:
Johnny, Matthew, Jacob, Allie, Katie,
Caroline, Jack and Noah.
These are some stories about your Gommie and Papa,
How we lived and what we believe to be important.

Preface

ᘓᘙ ᘚᘗ

"What has been will be again, what has been done will be done again…" (Ecclesiastes 1:9 NIV).

*B*ack to the Cottage: Leadership Wisdom for Today* is the story of my personal journey starting with a series of family "Cottage" businesses, continuing through corporate America and winding up in the "Information Age." During this journey I learned to apply leadership principles and techniques that, in many ways, I had learned in the Cottage of my youth. I have had the opportunity to test these leadership principles and techniques many times in a variety of organizations ranging from small to large, from profit to nonprofit, from American to International cultures. The principles and techniques I learned early on have adjusted to the technological and sociological changes of a much more vast and global economy, but interestingly, the core of what I learned years ago is still the core and when applied as such, it works.

We are now entering yet another age which some are labeling the "Entrepreneurial Age." Millions of individuals are trying to determine how to go back to the Cottage, to find a simpler and more consistent way to live and provide for their needs. This will be an exciting age, but not without difficulty. I offer my story as one of many that will be written and hopefully found useful for future generations to build on.

I want this book to provide a vision of what can be regarding leadership and organizational transformation... and also, a bit of the "how to." The book isn't exhaustive, but it offers enough know-how to help entrepreneurs get started and, perhaps more importantly, to realize that it isn't rocket science. Any ambitious leader can use these principles to embark on a path that will progress his or her organization. With commitment, leaders will be able to use *Cottage Leadership* to achieve the end objectives of their enterprise, no matter the nature of said goals.

A Look Back

In the 1960's, management thought-leaders described the transformation and operational improvement of large Industrial Age organizations with terms like socio-technical systems, team systems, high performance work systems, and total quality management. Reading breathless accounts of increased productivity and morale, young businesspeople might have imagined these were new-to-the-world attempts at engaging workers in greater participation with their organizations.

I had the wonderful advantage of working in a Fortune 500 company as it migrated from top-down management to full integration. I also had the advantage of growing up in a Cottage business, so I knew none of this was especially new. What I saw at work inside Procter and Gamble was an admirable, often skillful, reapplication of time-tested ideas from the Cottage.

In addition to my early training in family business and my experience with P&G, I was on an intellectual and spiritual quest to trace the threads of business, leadership and work in the ancient biblical narratives. The further I travelled these parallel journeys, the more I identified three significant truths:

1. There are a few core values that human beings really connect with; when leaders pay attention to these, they establish an excellent foundation for building capability in their organizations.
2. There are many more leaders in any organization than most people realize; when they all get on the same page—sharing the same core values and objectives—capacity is created that outstrips the imagination.
3. Business leaders have an interesting way of confusing or ignoring simple truths when faced with what they consider to be more important—or at least more pressing—issues and opportunities.

There was time when every private business endeavor was a Cottage industry—in much of the world this remains the case. National and global corporations have a great deal to learn from the Cottage (certainly more to learn than they have to teach at this point).

Back to the Cottage is the story of my odyssey from the Cottage to the corporation and back again. It chronicles the values and principles I learned in the Cottage business of my youth. I hope my tale sparks business leaders to test these values and principles. They'll learn how to create and enjoy major success by paying attention to seemingly minor details.

Chapter 1

Field Tested

ﾍ⋑ ⋐ﾍ

Six a.m. is a very quiet and peaceful time in the North Florida community of Perry, about 50 miles southeast of Tallahassee. This morning was no exception as I cooled down after my morning run. Dawn was breaking, birds and critters adding pleasant chatter to punctuate the silence, but I was far from peace myself. My head spun as I tried to understand what was happening to me—and not just me; it was happening to the thousand folks who reported to me at the local mill.

Less than 24 hours earlier, I learned that our corporate parent had decided we should leave the family. Well, that's what it felt like; actually, they were putting us up for sale and soon I would have to announce that news to the organization. Well aware of my feelings (disappointed and abandoned), what I didn't know—though I suspected— was how the others would react. How would this news affect the entire town, of which we were an integral part? The mill and the surrounding land for miles in every direction were involved in the sale. Our site was the economic lifeblood of this community, and all that was about to change.

My mind lurched from one episode to another as I thought back on the events of the past six years. Before then, the 50-year-old pulp mill in the middle of a million acres of planted pine and cypress swamps had deteriorated to the point that its future was uncertain. Profits were minimal and talk of selling the mill was clouded by the doubt that anyone would want it.

That was six years ago, when they brought me in to turn the mill around (if it could be turned). I'm happy to report that we pulled off a remarkable transition in every aspect of the business. We revitalized our technology, solidified the quality of our product base, and re-earned the loyalty of our customers while successfully weathering an environmental controversy that threatened the viability of our business. We reinvented the organization and spotlighted the skill-sets of our people. They transformed themselves from hourly shift workers into teams of competent, enthusiastic specialists. Our organization pulled together with a great deal of commitment. We had become profitable again—quite profitable!

As I ticked off these achievements in my mind it was difficult to square our success, and the promise of more, with the feeling that our corporate "mom and dad" were rejecting us. Oh, I knew the right words and would probably have to use them myself. "It's a business decision—this isn't personal." Well, it may not be personal at the corporate mother ship, but it sure was personal to me and, I suspected, to about 1000 others who worked with me!

Frankly, I wasn't sure I was up to the task of handing the mill over to new owners. The corporation had promised me another job after the transition, but they wanted me to provide onsite leadership until the business sold. There was no buyer in the wings; we would have to go through the whole process of visits, due diligence audits and negotiations until a sale could be completed. I wasn't sure I could do it.

The past six years had been an emotionally difficult succession of giddy highs and stomach-dropping lows. I valued peaks and valleys—along with the relationships they produced—but this? I didn't sign up for this. It seemed like the company was sending us in the wrong direction. Perhaps back where we were six years earlier. I saw myself as a builder, a restorer, a fixer—not a dismantler. Maybe it was time to move on, let someone else handle this new problem, or opportunity. No way in my mind was this an opportunity. Reeling—I was ready to give up.

Then a strange thing happened; an unexpected image entered my mind. I'm a fairly linear thinker. A new thought is usually linked to my previous thought. This one came out of the blue. I saw myself at the age of 16, standing in a field in upstate New York.

Slim Pickings

I grew up on a small farm where my parents operated a Cottage business. There was never a time when I wasn't involved in the family business—or businesses. We created value through a number of operations centered on the farm. When I was about twelve my father got me started in a small business of my own—sweet corn. It began as a garden patch and grew to several acres. Dad helped me plant in the late spring each year and then left me more or less on my own to farm the corn.

For all practical purposes I was the boss. My best friend Don was my hired hand during harvest time each August. Every morning we headed for the corn field at 5:00 a.m. to pick enough ears to supply the stand in front of our old farmhouse and six small stores in nearby towns. On days when sales were particularly brisk, we returned to the field several times to pick more.

We cultivated seven acres the year I turned sixteen. We staged the corn to ripen at different times through the picking season but about halfway through August several rows matured at the same time. It was more than we could sell through our market of six small stores and the stand in front of our house.

My father knew of a wholesale distributor in a city about 30 miles away. He called them and they placed an order for ten thousand ears of corn, to be delivered the next day. Ten thousand ears represented a mind-boggling amount of work to me. Until then, a big day was a thousand ears. I had no idea how to complete this task.

I was about to concede that I was in over my head, when my father asked, "Would you like some help?"

Two thoughts flashed through my mind. First, without a doubt I wanted and needed help. Second, my father was a strong individual and, whenever he got involved, he tended to have the final say. Saying "yes" would mean I had to give up being the boss. Still, it didn't take long to decide. I was out of my depth so I welcomed his help.

We headed for the field immediately—my father, my best friend and me. As we bumped along in the pickup, I thought about that day's work area. It was a really nice planting: tall stalks, no weeds, and large firm ears. I began to get excited about the challenge of it all, forming a strategy to pick more than Don. I assumed he wanted to out-pick me, as well. Neither of us liked losing and we both figured the key to winning was diving into the area of new growth.

When we parked, Don and I both grabbed our baskets and headed for the corn. But, my father stopped me and said, "John, why don't you pick over there..." Over there wasn't new growth; it was an area that had already been picked!

I thought my father was just confused—after all, he hadn't been involved that much, so how could he know? "Dad, we've already picked that area," I said. "There isn't any corn left!"

"I know it's been picked," he replied, "but there's more and we don't want to miss any."

About this point I wondered if my father knew what he was talking about, but I also knew my father. It wasn't a good idea to question him further. I'd go through the motions for a while, prove there was no corn, and then get on with the real picking. Meanwhile, I was losing valuable time while Don took the lead.

After piddling around for a few minutes I came back to where my father was picking with five or six ears in my basket. "Dad," I said, with some exasperation in my voice I'm sure. "There just isn't any corn over there. I've been really looking and this is all I found. Guess I'd better start picking over here with Don, right?"

Dad responded, "Oh, I think there's more corn there and we'll need it to fill this order. Come on, I'll go with you and take a look." He wasn't upset with me, but it was quite clear that he was set on thoroughly picking that area a second time.

So my father went with me and picked a basket-full in a fairly short time; not like in the new growth, but certainly faster than I thought possible. He'd made his point and I got busy. What amazed me was that I did start finding corn; it was as if I had been blind to it before. I really didn't want to be there, so I had closed myself off to the possibilities.

Later, when I joined Don in the new growth, it was easy picking. I never caught up with him, but we picked 10,000 ears that day and Dad was right about needing the corn we took out of the picked-over area. Without it we would have fallen short. So I felt good about what we accomplished together. I felt especially good the next day when Dad and I delivered the fruits of our labor to the "big city."

Don't Quit Before the Job is Done
Remembering that flashback so many years later in Perry, Florida, I thought, *Oh, those were the good ol' days, why can't life be that simple now?*

My next thought was: *You know, I'm in kind of a field now, and like that picked-over cornfield, I really don't want to pick here anymore. I want to get into some "new growth." But, like my father told me that day in the cornfield, "We don't want to miss any; we'll need it to fulfill our objective."*

What Dad was really saying was, "Don't quit now; don't quit before the job is done!" And I got it. That became a core value in my life. I couldn't quit now any more than I could as a 16-year-old. I had a responsibility and I had to see it through. People were counting on me.

So I made up my mind to keep on keeping on. I would do whatever was necessary to transform this problem into an opportunity. I'd do my best to make a successful transition for my team; then I would worry about myself.

That morning was one in a succession of moments that demonstrated how profoundly my early years in a Cottage industry affected me; raised by people who grew up in the Cottage tradition. The values they instilled have impacted me countless times. They make the difference still.

Tensions of Modern Business

It bears repeating: the values and principles I learned in the Cottage are conspicuous by their absence in much of the corporate world, as if they'd never been discovered, or were lost—or ignored. Yet, in some companies I have seen genuine efforts to be principles-based or values-based. Some merely paid lip service to the concept. Where those efforts have been faithfully and consistently played out I have seen good business results: sustained profits, resilience and adaptability in the face of marketplace changes in the unfolding of the Information Age.

Going forward, I am convinced we will need more of this values-based or principles-based approach in business— indeed in any realm where people gather to accomplish a common objective. This is especially true when we consider the growing tensions we face:

- Increasing pressure to create value quickly
- Industry consolidation—acquire or be acquired
- Short-term pressure to improve the bottom line, yet long-term need to position for the future
- Balancing financial results with ethical demands
- Maintaining product quality in the face of downward price pressure
- Attracting, developing, and retaining good people
- Developing a culture of collaboration in a fast-paced environment

I have come to believe that the core values and beliefs we adhere to, no matter the cost, are the foundation for our lives. They are the bedrock on which we build. They anchor us, guide us, and pull us together to accomplish impossible missions. The history of our civilization is filled with the stories of individuals, groups, and communities who built and achieved remarkable things. The common thread through all these stories follows the values and principles that sustained their vision, directed their steps, corrected their course and defined their success. Here and there, where we still see marvelous examples of people accomplishing great things together, they are very clear about their underlying values and principles. The opposite is also true: companies (of whatever sort) who don't agree on who they are and where they are going, end up lost in the woods.

I am not naïve about this. Plenty of family businesses have floated briefly then sunk without a trace. As the designer Clement Mok said, "The music is not in the piano." The music is in the people who embody the values and principles of the Cottage: my parents and grandparents; the designers and craftspeople who create beautiful, functional artifacts that make people's lives better; as well as manufacturers, distributors and retailers who insist on quality, equity and service throughout the value chain. The Cottage industries that succeeded in the past and are successful today share a common DNA of values and principles that bond people together and guide their direction and decision-making. It has never been perfect, but Cottage values are consistent. Many, perhaps most, abandoned those values in the Industrial Age, choosing instead the orthodoxies of progress and scientific management, which, to be fair, worked on a number of levels until they stopped working (more on that shortly). Today, many (perhaps most) are unfamiliar with the values of the Cottage, or uncertain about their robustness in the rapidly shifting world of commerce.

If we expect to deal with the tensions and opportunities we face just ahead I am convinced we must recover those Cottage values and the principles by which they are lived out in the workplace. I am convinced we can return to the Cottage (even those among us who have yet to learn those values and principles) and build strong business cultures that will carry us into the future. I hope the stories that follow will convince you too.

Chapter 2

The Cottage

Summer transitioned quickly to a dramatic fall in upstate New York. The air was cool and crisp, and the hillsides blazed with vivid reds, yellows and oranges encroaching on green patches still resisting the inevitable.

The white farmhouse sat in the middle of brightly colored maples on a bluff overlooking the Susquehanna River. Just behind the house was an aging red barn and a long shed that housed the shop. Off to the right sat the red sugarhouse.

A decrepit school bus dropped me in front of the house at 3:30 p.m. like clockwork. I imagine it was the same bus my Mom and Dad rode before me.

I was first off the bus, followed close behind by my younger sister Ellen. Our big collie—Lassie, if you can believe it—waited in the front yard to greet us. The three of us ran to the house where we were greeted, as always, by Mom and our youngest sister Barbie, who rode the earlier kindergarten bus. Mom, as usual, had snacks ready, and lots of questions for our daily school debriefing.

Mom the Scheduler doled out our tasks. "Ellen, the living room needs dusting and vacuuming, and Barbie, I'd like you to get your room cleaned up. Johnny, I think Dad's got some chores for you in the shop." All this was part of the routine, as was the knowledge that dinner would be ready promptly at 6:00 p.m., followed by homework and bedtime.

Lassie and I headed out of the house and across the graveled driveway to the long shed. I looked for Dad and Gramp in the shop they built for constructing handmade truck bodies. This was the mid-1950s and trucks were often purchased with just the chassis, engine and cab. Small shops like ours built custom aftermarket bodies. My dad and grandfather developed an excellent reputation for building high quality truck bodies. Their workmanship was so good it wasn't unusual for customers to have the bodies transferred to a second truck—a few even outlasted three trucks.

I opened the shop door and yelled, "Dad, where are you?"

Someone answered, "Hey Johnny, we're over here!" Over here was the back of the shop where two busy workers laid the floor for a new truck body. Don and Mickey were employees, but they seemed like family to me. I had known them my whole life and was as comfortable with them as I was with my father and grandfather.

As I approached, Don grinned at Mickey and tossed a nail back over his shoulder where it clinked on the floor. "Durn it Johnny. There's another one with the head on the wrong end!"

What Don didn't know is that Gramp had pulled the same gag on me a few days earlier—the same day he complained, "Johnny, I've cut this board three times and it's still too short!"

I played along with Don. "Maybe the guy who made those nails got up on the wrong side of the bed that day!" Another line courtesy of Gramp.

Mickey responded with a big horselaugh, tickled to see his work partner bested by a ten-year-old. Don was impressed enough with my comeback to let it rest. "Johnny, I 'spect you're right about that! Your dad and grandfather are in the pasture, down by the creek, putting the fence back together. Those Hereford yearlings got a little rambunctious this morning and knocked it down."

"Thanks," I said. "See you guys later." As I took off toward the pasture, Lassie trailed behind. I skirted around the sugarhouse—one of those buildings with what looked like another tiny house on the rooftop. The up-top house was actually a steam vent for the evaporators that cooked down the sweet maple sap we collected each spring to make syrup. Mom made a wonderful spread called maple cream, and my grandmother made little sugary maple candies, which they sold to provide additional family income.

As I rounded the building, I couldn't help thinking about those confections and my role in gathering sap from the trees scattered across our little farm. Several more men worked with us during that two-month season every year, tapping trees and gathering sap from farther out. We produced enough syrup each season to keep Mom busy making maple cream and Gram making candy the rest of the year. Dad delivered their products to specialty shops in the area. My mother handled the bookkeeping and payroll from a desk and file cabinet in an alcove off the kitchen where she integrated much of her work.

I found Dad and Gramp stretching a strand of barbed wire along a line of fenceposts, a couple of which looked new. As I ran up, Dad launched my second debriefing of the day. "Hi Bub, how was school today?" But Dad's questions were always easier; he required less information than Mom.

I restated what I told Mom earlier. Everything was fine. I got a better grade on my history test than expected. I bemoaned history class, soliciting sympathy from dad. "If I had my choice there'd be only math and science and baseball and football in school anyway. And no girls!" Dad said that made a certain amount of sense to him as well, but that if people didn't know history they were destined to repeat it.

I asked, "What happened to the fence?" It was Gramp who found the breech earlier that day. His pride and joy were loose — fourteen Hereford steers and cows. The mystery of their whereabouts was solved when a neighbor drove up to report the Herefords were down at his place. After some effort to drive them back to home pasture, Gramp recruited my dad, and they set about repairing the fence.

When I asked what he wanted me to do, my dad answered, "How about giving Gramp a hand on the other end of this wire? I think he's getting a little tired."

I ran down to where Gramp was pulling horseshoe-shaped nails from his lips and hammering the wire to a fencepost. Gramp hollered out of the side of his mouth, "Hey, Johnny boy, you sure are a sight for my tired eyes, I need some help! How about I hold this wire and you nail it, okay?" Gramp was doing just fine but he took every opportunity to get me involved. By age ten, I knew how to do things around the farm with which some grown men struggle.

I took the hammer, grabbed a nail from the bag at Gramp's feet, set the points above and below the taut wire to the right side of a barb and drove it into the post, securing the strand parallel to the ground. Gramp said, "Perfect Johnny, now go back along the fence and put a nail in each post." It felt so good being a "man" and the center of attention!

After dinner that evening, my dad headed out to Gram and Gramp's side of the big old farmhouse; something he did two or three times a week. I just finished my homework and decided to tag along. Times like this were special for me because they generally meant listening in on strategy talks about the family business. And whenever my father or grandfather realized they were discussing something I didn't understand, they took the time to explain it to me.

When it came time for storytelling (one of our favorite sources of entertainment) my mother, grandmother and sisters were usually present as well. I sat riveted whenever they told the story about the time Ellen and I played in the hayloft above the shed. When it happened, I was about five and a half and Ellen was four. As we horsed around the half empty loft, Ellen slipped on some loose hay and slid right out the small loft door.

At that very moment Mom was looking out the kitchen window and saw Ellen plummet to the gravel drive and lay there in a clump. Moments later Mom burst out the back door on a dead run, screaming as she came.

Dad heard the screaming from inside the shop. The first thing to cross his mind was that Mom had seen one of the rabid animals that inhabited their land in recent weeks. He grabbed his .22 rifle and headed toward the noise.

By this time, realizing my sister had disappeared, I headed down the back stairs to the ground floor of the shed. When I reached the gravel driveway I found my mother tending to Ellen; and just behind them stood my father with the rifle.

It turned out that Ellen was miraculously uninjured so Mom helped her up, dusted her off, and took her into the house. Watching them head up to the house, and being the farm kid that I was—remember, just five-and-a-half—I asked what seemed to me like the most obvious question. "Wuz ya gonna shoot her Dad?"

You don't get that question so much in the suburbs. But I had seen animals so badly hurt that my father or grandfather had to put them down, as we say in the country. Having not yet fully understood the rules of engagement, I thought it made perfect sense to ask for clarification—which my father gladly provided.

"Putting Ellen down" was just one of several great stories we'd recount for nighttime entertainment. Bedtime came after the stories. Morning arrived ahead of the sun on our little farm, as it did for most folks in rural America. About the time others get to work, Dad and Gramp stopped for breakfast and a second cup of coffee. Gramp often declared the day was half over by 8:00 in the morning. Although my sisters and I didn't have to get up quite so early, we had chores to do before the school bus came, and it wasn't unusual for me to be up and at 'em early on non-school days to help Dad or Gramp. Sleeping-in was nonexistent in our household.

The unwritten norm in our family was "get the work done and then play all you want." My primary objective at that point in life was playing ball—baseball, football, or basketball—depending on the time of year. If I had to do a little work first in order to do what I loved, that was fine by me; I'd just get it behind me, then get on with what I considered to be the important things in life.

This formative life educated me more than my proper academics. The values and principles instilled by my family, work, play, and spiritual development grew with me as I became a man.

I was the first in my family to go to college. Although no one acknowledged it at the time, I suppose we all knew that when I left for school it would be the first time that an oldest son in my family would not return to carry on the family business.

I spent a few more summers taking care of the vegetable business, but in reality the seed was sown for a more radical change. I wasn't just leaving behind an economic model of production and distribution, I left a culture—a way of life. It would be some time before I understood the loss, and began my journey back to the Cottage.

Chapter 3

Cottage Principles

My story reflects the dynamics and characteristics associated with traditional Cottage industry—a business form typically, and I think erroneously, assumed to have petered out with the Industrial Revolution. There have always been mom & pop businesses, and I imagine there always will be. The commercial well curve that became apparent in the 2000 US Census is evidence that it's not Cottage businesses that are being squeezed out of the economy but mid-sized companies. The digital age means just about anyone can do almost anything from nearly anywhere by keeping quality, innovation and service high and overhead low. Competing with nimble little guys on speed, price and quality is as tough as taking on economic heavyweights. It may never have been more dangerous to be stuck in the middle of the market than now.

But it's dangerous everywhere. The age of patronage from big corporations is over. Like or lump it, with rare exception it is irrefutably true. Being a company man seemed like a safe proposition for just about one generation, and I don't mean the one of which you are a part. Forget about playing by the corporate rules; the rules have changed and there's very little anyone can do about that. Today, the position of workers at every level in big business is at risk.

If I am right about what is in the rest of this book, our refuge may not be adapting to a new set of corporate rules but re-learning the lessons of the Cottage.

Looking back on my own return to the Cottage, I can identify seven values I learned from Mom and Dad, Gram and Gramp and the others who took part in our business. These values are the basis of what I value in the business life.

1. The Value of Knowing What You Stand For

Webster's dictionary defines principles as deeply held beliefs or strong convictions about something. Psychologists say that what we have strong convictions about really determines who we are, how we behave, and ultimately what we will become. Our principles function as a foundation for our lives. For better or worse, everyone believes something and behaves according to a set of principles, whether they consciously realize it or not.

My home environment embodied a set of principles that passed through our family for several generations. I experienced these principles in the day-to-day-ness of our family business—mostly from my parents and grandparents but also from individuals like Mickey and Don who worked in the business. One of these principles was the dedication to quality. My father's motto was wrapped up in a statement I heard many times, "If it's worth doing it's worth doing right."

He brought this home to me when I was about twelve. I was making a wooden jewelry box for my sister, Ellen. I had it assembled and sanded and, thinking it was good to go, I asked Dad for the stain. He said, "Got it ready to go, eh Bub? Let me see how it looks!" He took a careful look at it and said, "This is a really good looking jewelry box Johnny, but it needs more sanding before you apply the finish." He must have noted my discouraged look—after all this was for my sister. Did it need to be so perfect? "Always remember son, if it's worth doing, it's worth doing right."

Was Dad ahead of his time? It seems to me that industry didn't really get it until the Total Quality Management systems of the 1980s. Or, like so many things, was quality part of our business culture all along (at least in the Cottage) that fell into neglect in the mainstream?

The value of knowing what you stand for—this principle was evident in the truck bodies and the maple syrup, cream, and candy our family made. And it was obvious in the vegetable business my father helped me launch to earn money for college. The standard he advised me to establish was simple: sell only freshly picked corn. Every morning I replaced corn not sold the previous day with fresh picked ears. The standard was faithfully applied at the stand in front of the house and for all stores we supplied. We did it even though day old corn is really not that bad and even though it meant more waste than most farmers were willing to incur. Sticking to the principle served us well. Our reputation for quality enabled us to sell all the corn we raised at good prices. In the process, I learned just in time inventory replenishment in the 1950s. Life in the Cottage was so advanced!

Knowing what we stand for, our principles, governs how we behave—how we do business. The most successful Cottage industries I observed as a youngster were led by patriarchs and matriarchs who worked from a set of strongly held beliefs about how things ought to be. They never wavered, even though the temptation to do so was great, and even when their principles threatened the bottom line.

I remember hearing the motto of a ship builder who said, "We will build great ships—at a profit if we can, at a loss if we must—but we will build great ships." This could certainly have been a motto for my father and grandfather.

There came a time in the truck body business when it was no longer possible to maintain quality and compete with the mass-produced bodies from the big corporations. Dad and Gramp could easily have taken shortcuts; they could have built lower quality bodies. Instead, they decided to move on to the next venture, which, for them, was expanding the maple syrup business to compete in a ready market. The one thing they never did was compromise the principle: "If it's worth doing, it's worth doing right."

2. The Value of Knowing Where You Are Going

It's amazing how often I encounter business leaders whose annual reports, disguised by layers of carefully constructed copy, might as well be: "We have no idea where we're going but we're getting there 8½ percent more efficiently than the same period last year!"

The Cottage industry may lack many things that we enjoy in larger companies but one thing it doesn't lack is a sense of direction and purpose. Everyone connected with our family's business understood exactly what had to be accomplished, both in a macro and a micro sense. I got it as a ten-year-old kid; my mother and grandmother knew it; the people hired by my father and grandfather were even familiar with it. That shared understanding was necessary in order for the business to succeed. Every one of us was aware of all aspects of the business. We comprehended the beginning inputs, we realized the end objective, and we knew the middle process where the product was created. We understood exactly what the others counted on us to deliver.

Today we talk about the need for the leader to know where he or she is going. In the Cottage it is necessary for everyone to know. When my father and grandfather left the shop to mend the fence, Mickey and Don needed no instruction. They knew the objective of their work and they knew what had to be done next. They also recognized that their income depended on the success of the business. Dad and Gramp didn't have to worry about Mickey and Don sloughing off while they were gone; I don't remember my father or grand-father ever being concerned about their employees working hard. When no one needs micromanaged, everyone feels like they have an integral part in the overall success of the project, and everyone is used to their full capacity.

3. The Value of Honesty and Integrity

Honesty and integrity form the primary route to trust and a trustworthy reputation. Trust is the glue that holds relation-ships together. Success in the Cottage requires trust between all those connected to it as owners, employees, suppliers, and customers.

My father and grandfather would never dream of cutting corners, nor would they allow any of the rest of us to do so. They would never dream of telling a small fib, like prom-ising they could deliver something by a certain date in order to get business when they knew they really couldn't. When my father or grandfather made a commitment people knew it was as good as done.

I don't believe this was true just in our family—any family engaged in any type of Cottage business has to prac-tice honesty and integrity or risk going out of business.

4. The Value of Planning

Knowing where you are going requires that you also know how you will get there. Planning implies a systematic approach—a series of steps or a road map to the destina-tion. In previous times, Cottage industries may not have had the kind of documentation and computerized planning tools available to big corporations, but they certainly had system-atic approaches for everything they did. These days, anyone with a computer has access to off-the-shelf digital planning tools that would astound my parents and grandparents.

My father had a template for every type of truck body he built. He maintained an accurate inventory of parts, many of which he also fabricated. He knew exactly what had to be done to build a truck body, how long it should take and the cost of each part of the process. Unless they were very new, anyone who worked for my father knew the same things. Any one of them could step up to virtually any situation and handle it. As a consequence, our basic operations were quite smooth—with little variance and few mistakes.

I believe this is true throughout successful Cottage industries. When I look at the quality and precision in old furniture, glassware, jewelry, timepieces and the like, I see the implementation of planning, systems, and carefully calculated approaches.

One thing a plan should not imply is that it is the only way to do things—that there is never a need to change. On the contrary the value of planning means taking into account the inevitability of change, and planning for that as well.

5. The Value of Each Individual

Each individual in the Cottage is critical; whether it's literally just Mom and Pop, or Mom and Pop plus several more. A small business cannot afford to support even one person who doesn't pull his weight.

I have no doubt that different management styles probably existed in Cottage industries, ranging from controlling and directing every move to a more empowering coaching and development style. My suspicion, however, is that Cottage business leaders who develop their people are more successful in the long run—especially when it comes to exiting the business through succession or sale.

My father and grandfather certainly saw it that way. Dad, in particular, went out of his way to show others how to master an operation or develop a skill. He balanced great patience with a demand for excellence. He was very aware of the differences among people and seemed to have a knack for seeing each worker's potential. A man by the name of Walt worked with my father in our maple syrup business— by nature a seasonal business with most of the activity in the late winter and early spring. This fit Walt's rhythm to a T because he drove heavy equipment for road construction, a seasonal business undertaken primarily in the summer months in upstate New York.

Walt was a quick learner and Dad eventually taught him all he knew about the maple syrup business. This proved to be a very valuable investment. The process of making maple syrup involves boiling off the water until the right consistency is reached. The amount of water that has to be vaporized is huge (forty gallons for each gallon of maple syrup), and at the peak my father made over five thousand gallons of syrup each season. Walt became Dad's right arm in the business; they became so close that Walt started thinking like my father.

Once the maple sap started flowing, there were times when it ran steadily from the trees for several days. This required boiling 24 hours a day for days on end. My father always took the night shift and let Walt handle days, which was also the time for most of the ancillary activities; things like moving fuel and maintaining equipment. That's how much confidence Dad had in Walt—and the whole team for that matter.

Dad believed in giving everyone a chance, training them in as many different skills as they could handle, and turning them loose to do what they were equipped to do. He didn't look over people's shoulders and when we made mistakes he patiently helped us learn from them. He didn't tolerate the same mistake over and over—everyone understood that. It was also understood that he wanted us to treat mistakes as learning opportunities.

The result was that even though most of our work was seasonal and part-time, my father always had his pick of good people. They wanted to work for him because they knew he placed high value on each person and gave significant opportunities to contribute to the enterprise, not to mention the expanded skill set most of our workers gained. I can't imagine anyone being less employable as a result of working in our Cottage business.

6. The Value of Teamwork

There is an old Hebrew proverb found in scripture that reads: "Two are better than one because they have a good return for their work. If one falls down his friend can help him up. But pity the man who falls and has no one to help him up!" (Ecclesiastes 4:9-10, New International Version).

Cottage industry is rarely a one-man show. Generally speaking, there is at least Mom and Pop. I never realized how much my mother and father were a team until my father passed away. It was then that I realized the extent of the team-work. Mom, as it turned out, was the business manager, and Dad was the creative, product development partner. Oh, they both knew all of the business and could fill in for the other, but they each had their special areas of skill and knowledge.

In fact, everyone who worked in our little family enterprise had to be a team player—none of this "it's not my job" stuff. Whoever was closest to the mess (or the opportunity) was expected to handle it, unless it was dangerous and the person hadn't been trained for it. The ethos was to share the work, both pleasant and the unpleasant.

I remember those days in late winter when we tapped the maple trees just before the sap began to rise. Typically, there was deep snow in the woods so everything had to be done on snowshoes. Tapping in the 1950s included someone with a gas-powered engine strapped on his back to drive a hand drill. He slogged from tree to tree, drilling holes about 5 or

6 inches into each one. A second person came behind and drove a spile into the hole through which the sap dripped. A third person attached a bucket beneath the spile and a fourth slid a cover onto the top of the bucket to keep out snow and rain. Two more workers kept the first four supplied with spiles, buckets, and covers.

What I remember is how smoothly it always seemed to go. Of the crew, four could do any of the tasks, and then there would be a schoolboy or two (like me) learning by helping out. The original version of on-the-job training. Those who could do it all rotated frequently to keep things interesting, and prevent tiring as quickly. I don't recall anyone ever barking orders. They just knew what to do and, when it was time, they did it.

Cottage industries are small operations. They have only a few people to make the whole business go. There is no room for specialization. Everyone has to be a "jack of all trades," and they must do high quality work or risk losing out to someone who does it better. Teamwork and sharing the load are essential to mutual success.

7. The Value of Continual Learning and Improvement

As the saying goes, "We are either improving or regressing. There is no status quo." Understanding this principle has been one difference between success and failure throughout the ages. Cottage industry no doubt has its share of both, and it may be that the demise of many small businesses is ultimately a failure to learn and improve.

My grandfather started in the early 1900s with a dairy business—producing milk, butter, and cheese, delivered to your door. By 1940 the family farm was too small to support the business, so Gramp and my dad began raising chickens.

This lasted about 10 years until the chicken business no longer provided enough income on its own. They transitioned to building truck bodies, which provided well for our family for another decade.

Throughout the years, beginning with my grandfather, maple syrup was a small side crop. In the early 1960s Dad and Gramp figured they could turn syrup into a profitable business by purchasing sap from local farmers and boiling it down to produce syrup, candy and maple cream for market. So they went to work on the idea.

Dad was pretty clever and invented several pieces of equipment to take this business to scale — plus he and Gramp always had a nose for good deals in used equipment. The long and short of it is, they put together a pretty good business, and did it all with used or invented equipment and an old-fashioned pay-as-you-go philosophy.

By 1980, my grandfather had passed on, and I was well into an industry career. It became clear that I would not be taking over the family business, and Dad had just about run out of gas with the maple syrup operation. We all agreed it was time to sell off most of the assets and downsize the business to a level he could comfortably handle by himself.

But that's not the end of the story. Back in the 1950s, when Dad and Gramp stopped raising chickens they had to decide what to do with the land. For the first few years they raised cash crops: grain, sweet corn, and string beans. This was how I became involved in the sweet corn business in my teenage years. Around 1965 my father converted the acreage to another venture: Christmas trees. By the time he decided to downsize the maple business, he had a small but flourishing Christmas tree business. Dad managed that business until he passed on in 1993; my mother kept it going until 1997; today my sister and her husband are doing very well with the same business.

The point of all of this is that my grandfather and my father never stopped learning about new possibilities and never stopped trying things in an effort to improve the business. They didn't wait for a catastrophe or a downturn to force them to react. They always had the next venture under development and at the appropriate time they moved on it. True, they never succeeded at creating a big business, but that was never their objective. Their objective was to operate a business that offered something worthwhile, to do it in a way they could be proud of, and to earn enough money to support two families and have a little left over to pass along to the next generation. In this respect I believe they were wildly successful.

Seven Key Cottage Values
- The Value of Knowing What You Stand For
- The Value of Knowing Where You Are Going
- The Value of Honesty and Integrity
- The Value of Planning
- The Value of Each Individual
- The Value of Teamwork
- The Value of Continual Learning and Improvement

I believe these are the seven key values or characteristics of Cottage industry. I won't suggest that these characteristics are always present in every Cottage enterprise—history tends to favor the ones that succeeded over those that failed. But, when I consider my own experience and when I look at what those little businesses were (and are) capable of producing, I am convinced these are the values that make the Cottage model work.

Chapter 4

Shuttering the Cottage

৵৩ৄ ৄৄ৵

The notion of Cottage business suggests novelty and quaintness—the absence of standardization. Generally, when people think of Cottage industry, they think of the 1800's and earlier; before industrialization and steam-powered transportation made manufactured goods comparatively cheap and available to a widespread market.

The advent of power systems: steam, electricity, and the gasoline engine, opened the possibility of developing machines and manufacturing processes to mass produce and distribute products that had previously been built—if they were built at all—one at a time and delivered locally. New products, like the automobile, electric lights, and the radio were often prototyped in Cottage settings but could be produced affordably only when scaled for mass production. Industrialization made textiles uniform and dirt-cheap. In Europe, machines allowed products to be created with shorter turnaround times than ever before. In North America, Henry Ford prototyped the efficiencies of assembly line manufacturing, and then paid his workers the remarkable sum of $5 dollars a day so they could become his customers.

All of this revolutionized economic life and the social order—but it came with a price. It devalued our perception of each individual. The age of machines enabled large factories employing hundreds and even thousands of workers and required new thinking about maintaining order to get things done. "Management" was born and, strangely I think, much of what had gone on in the Cottage for thousands of years was tossed—the baby with the bathwater.

Of course, new technology required new thinking. Bosses had to contend with the complexities of huge factories and newfangled machines churning out newly invented products. Probably the biggest issue managers faced was the influx of workers from farm communities and other countries, drawn by the promise of steady work at favorable wages. Culture clashes were inevitable.

Losing Cottage Values

Frederick Taylor came up with the first widely known management theory—scientific management. Taylor was tagged the "Father of Industrial Engineering." The essence of this theory was that, for any manufacturing process, a few managers should plot out each step along with plans to accomplish each step. They trained each worker to complete just one of those steps and monitored individuals to be certain they did the task exactly as prescribed. Taylor theorized that if a worker didn't have to think about what he was doing, he would be happier, which would result in a more efficient work environment.

Perhaps one can't argue with this approach as a starting point—they had to start somewhere. But we know now that the theory evolved into a dysfunctional management style that tended to be highly autocratic at the expense of worker-investment. Very little thinking was encouraged (or even accepted) below the executive levels, which made workers feel less invested in the process and the product. Workers and lower level managers did what they were assigned and no more. Each person's operation was limited to his little job classification box.

Values esteemed highly in Cottage Industry disappeared (except at the top levels perhaps). Ideals faded, such as knowing where you're going (focus and direction), team-work (working together rather than work hierarchy), as well as continual learning and improvement by each worker. Over time, the trust level deteriorated between the lower and upper levels of organizations. This paved the way for the labor union movement because workers, feeling they had absolutely no voice, dared not trust management to keep their best interests at heart.

We continue to see the residual effects of this management philosophy today, in spite of attempts over the past 30 years to change. This doesn't stop at manufacturing—it became the norm in business. An assessment of most office-oriented organizations will reveal the same kinds of productivity and worker v. management issues.

Against the backdrop of this dismal picture there are promising stories. Some business leaders came to believe there is more to human nature than they realized earlier. Some managers discovered pre-industrial ways of working that have relevance in a progressively post-industrial world of work. In effect some have returned to the Cottage! Not in a physical sense of course (though the information age provides that opportunity in some cases), but in the sense of bringing forward the key values and characteristics of the Cottage.

Making the switch from top-down management back to the principles of family-based business is vital. Here are two stories to illustrate it, from personal experience.

Returning to the Family Business

My grandfather passed down a business legacy to family members. I've already outlined the evolution of the business to the point that my sister and her husband operated it as a successful Christmas tree farm. After my mother passed away in 1997, my other sister and her husband returned to the farm when he retired after many years with IBM. When IBM asked my brother-in-law to come out of retirement, he negotiated a deal to wire the farmhouse and return to what he did for years, rarely leaving the farm to consult with them. (Interesting enough, around this same time, telecommuting started becoming more popular as a work-at-home option.)

With the upgrade of the old farmhouse, my two sisters decided to establish yet another business, a craft shop, on the property. By my count that makes business number eight since my grandfather purchased the land in 1920. I think we will see more and more of this in the future, as information technologies provide opportunities to literally return to the Cottage.

Proctor & Gamble (My Employer for nearly 30 years)

P&G started off as a Cottage industry. Here is as excerpt from the book, *Eyes on Tomorrow* (Oscar Schisgall, J.G. Furguson Publishing, Chicago, 1981, page viii) about the growth and evolution of the company.

> "In the spring of 1837 two earnest men in their mid-thirties worked day after day in the yard behind their small shop in Cincinnati. Lean, black-bearded William Procter and the shorter, clean-shaven James Gamble stirred boiling animal fats in a large iron kettle slung over a wood fire. The fats were essential ingredients of the soap and candles they manufactured; products that William Procter himself would later deliver to local customers in a wheelbarrow."

Fifty years later, in 1887 (almost 30 years before Taylor issued his scientific management approach), P&G entered the industrial age and produced hundreds of thousands of soap bars each year. But they hadn't forgotten their roots. The leader of the company at that time was William Cooper Procter, grandson of William Procter. Read part of his philosophy given in a speech to the employees:

> "The first job we have is to turn out quality merchandise that consumers will buy and keep on buying. If we produce it efficiently and economically, we will earn a profit, in which you will share. But the profits can't be distributed unless they are earned." (*Eyes on Tomorrow*, page 49)

The younger Procter remembered his grandfather's values, either because he hung around the Cottage in the early days or because his father and grandfather influenced him. The fact is William Cooper Procter valued the employees and he "cut them in." When I worked for the company 100 years later, his values were still evident in employee loyalty, born from a trust that P&G paid attention to what mattered to all stakeholders.

In the 1960s Procter & Gamble began another industry leading effort. Having fallen into some of the same industrial revolution practices as other manufacturers, P&G suffered dismal results in the startup of a new soap plant. As they conducted a postmortem on the plant opening in the light of emerging organizational and motivational theory, they realized the factor that contributed most to failure was a missing "all-out commitment" from the employees.

This evaluation resulted in a fresh approach that included many of the values and characteristics true to P&G in their Cottage years. At the core was a sincere desire and effort to involve every person to their fullest potential and capabilities. Part of this strategy included a team approach that facilitated the interdependence so vital to success in the Cottage.

Above all, managers shifted their focus to become more like coaches, developing and encouraging individuals and teams to continually improve performance. It was as if the company had returned to its roots by embracing Cottage values and characteristics.

Subsequent plant startups performed beautifully and the new "old" approach was eventually rolled out to the whole company. Throughout its history, P&G has been willing to reinvent itself, which sometimes meant revisiting an important principle from the past. I'm convinced this is one reason, spanning three centuries, P&G continues to be one of America's largest companies.

Progress Means Pursuing Cottage Values

I understand that my list of seven Cottage values may not totally represent all Cottage industries that ever existed, but I'm convinced they are representative of the core values of most successful businesses. Based on this success rate, I propose we draw from the values and principles of the Cottage to facilitate a more effective outcome for tomorrow's opportunities.

This is possible in big business units as well as small companies—it works cross-platform. I've been a part of making it happen for various sized companies throughout my career. This old school approach is rare, because it appears to conflict with the contemporary penchant to manage by the numbers—and short-term numbers at that. The conflict is mainly in appearances only.

The rest of this book sets out to prove how the values of the Cottage are good in both a cultural sense as well as good for business. My goal is to show you that these values are, without doubt, the best way to create organizations capable of remaining effective at the rapid, globalized pace we'll all be working in from here forward.

Chapter 5

From the Cottage to the Corporation

꿏꿎 ꙓꙔ

T he alarm went off at 5:00 a.m. in our old farmhouse. But I wasn't a kid anymore so I hit the snooze button and started to roll over for another few minutes of sleep. Then it dawned on me—my wife Kathie and I were driving to Mehoopany, Pennsylvania that morning. It was 1967, two days before the New Year, and I was scheduled for a job interview with The Charmin Paper Products Company. We lived in Ohio, where I worked for Dupont, but I sought a new opportunity. We celebrated our first Christmas at home with our newly born daughter Kim and then drove to New York. I had scheduled the Charmin interview to coincide with a trip to see my parents.

The night before we had a fender bender coming in from Ohio and I was in no mood to get up early and drive another two hours—especially to interview with a company I had never heard of in a town called Mehoopany—population 300. Mehoopany was fun to say, but would anyone really want to live there? To make matters worse, I looked out the bedroom window and discovered snow falling.

Kathie stirred. "What time is it, honey?"

"It's 5:00 a.m.," I whispered. "But you don't need to get up. It's snowing and we're not going." At that point I didn't much care whether I had the job interview or not. I figured Kathie would be okay with that.

I was wrong. Kathie didn't just roll over and go back to sleep. She sat up and said, "What do you mean? You have a job interview!"

So I gave her my rationale, how I wasn't all that excited about a job in the "wilds" of Pennsylvania, and we probably couldn't get there anyway with all the snow. Normally, Kathie would agree with that logic, at least the snow part. But there have been a few instances in our life together when she has gone against what I thought was logical. This was one of them. She said, "Well, why don't we give it try—maybe it will be all right. If it isn't, we can always turn back."

We got up, dressed, and after a quick breakfast with my parents, headed out in their Chevy station wagon. We were the first ones on the road that passed my parents' farm and the big vehicle cut a fresh track in the six-inch accumulation. Once we made it to the main road we found the snowplow had been there ahead of us. The two-hour trip took three hours that morning, but we arrived safely and made several important discoveries along the way.

The first discovery was about five miles before we got to Mehoopany. We passed through a town called Tunkhannock, nestled between the Susquehanna River and the Endless Mountains of Pennsylvania. With fresh snow hanging in the trees it was as picturesque as a New England postcard. This scenic niche turned out to be where most of the Charmin managers lived.

The second discovery came as we drove up to the Charmin Paper site. I expected a smelly old paper mill but what we found instead was a huge and impressive new facility. It was clear I had done zero research on this outfit—more testimony to my sorry attitude.

The final discovery came during the interview when I learned that Charmin Paper Products was a relatively new subsidiary of the renowned Procter and Gamble Company. The more I learned the more I liked the whole deal. It was an opportunity to get in on the ground floor of something new, yet it had the backing of a major U.S. company.

I left Mehoopany with a major attitude adjustment— toward the Charmin Paper Products Company as well as the entire state of Pennsylvania.

I also left wondering if I even had a chance at the job. I had arrived unprepared and could only hope it wasn't too evident during the interview. We returned to Ohio just after New Year's Day and were greeted with a letter inviting me to return to Charmin for a follow-up interview.

The net of the story is I was hired to begin a new career with Procter and Gamble as a team manager at Charmin Paper Products. I didn't understand exactly what being a team manager meant, but I knew I would be a line-manufacturing manager in a brand new facility owned by a respectable Fortune 50 Company. Kathie was excited about the prospect of living in Tunkhannock. Nothing else mattered. I was excited to get started.

Learning and Growing

I began my Procter and Gamble career in March of 1968. After an orientation-training period I was assigned as a team manager in the Pampers disposable diaper manufacturing area. P&G essentially invented the disposable diaper. This was early in the process of this major profit-maker for the company, and I was thrilled to help make history.

My first boss was Wayne Richards, an All-Conference basketball player from Georgia Tech. At 6'7" tall, Wayne was the tallest man I had ever known. He was also the most interesting man I had ever known.

I played sports through high school and college without ever running into a coach quite like Wayne. He took me under his wing and showed me I was someone special. If I screwed up because I wasn't paying attention or trying hard enough, he had the ability to make me feel so bad I was determined never to let it happen again. But if I messed up while trying my best, he encouraged me to go for it again, and I would. When I got it right he made me feel ten feet tall—and I couldn't wait to succeed again (and again).

I wound up doing very well with Procter and Gamble and, in addition to what I owe for the values and principles I learned in my family's Cottage business, I owe a great deal of my success to Wayne Richards.

As a team manager I was responsible for a group of technicians operating a pair of disposable diaper manufacturing lines. If anyone on the team had a work-related accident, I was required to give a verbal presentation about the accident in the monthly management meeting. The plant employed over 2000 people with a management/professional group of about 300 strong, roughly half of whom attended each management meeting.

Eventually, my turn came to present the accident report. I had notes to show how the accident occurred and what steps we were taking to assure it wouldn't happen again. I stood up to speak to what seemed at the time like a huge group of managers. I felt like a child standing before these giants of P&G management—and I froze! I simply could not speak. Try as I might, the best I could get out was a sort of stutter. Finally I hung my head and sat down as Wayne took over, I was embarrassed and convinced I had sealed my fate with the great Procter and Gamble Company. At age twenty-four I knew I wouldn't have much of a career in management if I couldn't speak publicly.

After what seemed an eternity, the meeting ended and I slunk out like a whipped dog. But, I didn't get far. Wayne chased me down and pulled me aside to talk privately. This man who could scorch wallpaper off the wall when he was angry spoke to me in a way that made me believe I could over-come this flaw. "John," he said, "I understand what happened to you today. I also have difficulty speaking in public. I'm not going to let this stop your career, and you aren't either. We're going to work on this together until you get it right, okay?"

What could I say but "Yes sir!" Of course I had no idea what that would entail. From that day on Wayne pushed me to speak in public. He made me do presentations I didn't want to do—many times to visiting VIPs. He took a chance on me—again and again. Talk about putting your money where your mouth is!

At times, Wayne was unmerciful in his criticism. Other times he praised me more than I probably deserved. He had a great sense of timing—he knew when to push me, and when I was saturated with criticism. He coached me until I over-came my fear of public speaking. Perhaps most importantly, I learned more about coaching itself from that experience than from anything else in my career.

Procter and Gamble already had quite a tradition of coaching and mentoring new people. It was quite informal back then, but it worked well as a development tool. I found myself coaching others just getting started. At one point I counted over thirty individuals I coached early on who made it to the plant manager level or higher in the company. In many respects, coaching others to succeed is the accomplishment with which I'm most satisfied.

It is hard to overstate how fortunate I was to be at this particular plant in Pennsylvania. That's where Procter and Gamble solidified an understanding of how to develop truly empowered and productive organizations.

The process began a few years earlier as P&G started up a new soap plant in Augusta, Georgia. The management team utilized some early thinking about team-based organizations and genuinely invited the hourly work force to get involved in the management and operation of the business. It worked. In fact it worked very well, and it was only natural to extend those basic ideas and concepts as the company started up new facilities.

The next plant to open was this paper operation in Mehoopany. Some of the managers in the Augusta startup were drafted to join ones like Wayne Richards who came in from other P&G locations.

When I began, teams were already in place in every aspect of the business. Pay scale and progression in the company were based on each person's contribution through the number of specific skills he or she could successfully apply to accomplish business objectives. Managers were more like coaches than the "direct and control" leaders prevalent in industry up to that point.

My specific responsibility was managing a team of fourteen hourly employees—we called them technicians—who worked on a rotating shift schedule. Ours was one of four teams whose objective was to start up a brand new Pampers manufacturing department. Wayne Richards was our department manager. I had no prior management experience. My team was all new hires with the exception of three technicians who volunteered from departments started the previous year. With all the inexperienced staff, we were a little light on working knowledge.

Intently working together was the only way we could succeed. Though we lacked many technical skills, we quickly became a real team. I learned that the best help I could give was managing boundaries. That meant spending most of my time removing barriers and making sure the team had what it needed to get the job done. I also made sure each team member had a clear picture of what he or she needed for success; including the training or experience necessary to do the job. In short, I learned to coach.

I also learned a valuable lesson about managing in situations where I am not the most knowledgeable individual on the team. Even though no one had much expertise on this particular process, some had a great deal more knowledge (not to mention ability) on specific tasks than me. I found that leadership was the place where I could make the greatest contribution—not as a function of knowing the most but as a function of influencing others to accomplish worthy objectives. In that team I came to see that I had that ability—leadership was my part to play.

As time passed I had the opportunity to develop that ability in a variety of situations and locations. P&G's paper business soared, so there were many new plants to start up and a steep learning curve on products. After four years at Mehoopany, my family and I moved to Albany, Georgia where I functioned as startup department manager. From there we moved to Belleville, Ontario, Canada where I was the startup operations manager for a new diaper plant, and then we returned to the Albany plant where I served as startup manager for a new tissue unit and after that a new paper machine.

As this growth continued, Procter & Gamble was "Exhibit A" of what was becoming known as "High Performance Organizations." The emphasis was on teamwork (getting every team member to participate to the fullest potential) and a coaching style of leadership. Prior to every startup we studied the last several startups to develop an organizational design that extended and improved on all our previous efforts. In most cases our intentions were realized. We learned a tremendous amount about people and organizational behavior.

Albany, Georgia (like many southern cities), has a history of racial strife. We determined to hire a work force that reflected the racial makeup of the community and Albany became a case study on how we dealt with a racially diverse people group. When we announced the starting pay rate in the local newspaper, our plant manager, John Feldman, was summoned to an emergency meeting of the Chamber of Commerce. The starting rate was higher than the local norm, which was naturally a concern for other employers. But their primary concern was that we announced only one starting rate—instead of the traditional tiered rates for whites, blacks and women.

I don't think John made any friends at The Chamber that day. He believed in the P&G principle of treating everyone equally and he stood his ground. Word spread.

Several weeks later we had hired the first 100 people and were training them. I had a maintenance manager and three team managers scheduled to lead a five-day, three-shift schedule, and a few other staff managers helped me with the training. On Day One, one of the team managers, Bob Cary, greeted each of the hundred new employees by name. He had personally interviewed about half of them during the hiring process. He memorized the rest of the names by studying photographs. The rest of us were awestruck. We didn't do as well as Bob, but we worked hard to learn every name and get acquainted with each new employee. It's no exaggeration to say the new workers were amazed by the personal touch.

The first week was marked by high quality training and caring. As the end of the week approached I wondered what would happen the following Monday morning. Albany natives had been quick to warn us that many of our new employees probably wouldn't show up on Monday. They said that was the norm for Albany, especially among African American workers. I decided not to wait until Monday to find out.

As we wrapped things up on Friday afternoon, I addressed the entire group: "I've been told that many workers in Albany are undependable on Mondays—that they don't show up." I could see I had their undivided attention, but I had to wonder about the wisdom of what I was doing. Oh well, too late to turn back. "I want you to tell me what I should expect," I said. "Will all of you be here Monday morning?"

Immediately, one of the older African American men, George Lewis, stood up. I had no idea what to expect. He said, "John, up to now, no one has really cared whether we show up on Monday—or any other day for that matter. And up to now nobody has shown interest in us as people like y'all have. You can count on all of us being here on Monday and for as long as you need us." George sat down as the rest of the group murmured their collective agreement.

I didn't know what else to do, so I just said, "Thanks for a great first week. I look forward to seeing y'all [didn't take long to learn 'y'all'] on Monday."

We were amazed and excited about our first week. Something great had just taken place—we were in for a good ride as we put together this organization over the next few months. Years later it became obvious that Albany had become one of the company's finest facilities—and it continues today as a model of racial harmony in an area known more for racial discord.

I began to think I was destined to be a startup manager for the rest of my life when they assigned me to the position of plant manager for the Albany paper plant (Bounty towels, Charmin and White Cloud tissue). I served in that role for about a year before P&G asked me to take the same position for their large facility in Euskirchen, Germany.

Around this time I began to make the connection between what we did as an organization in these new businesses with the Cottage industry of my youth. I recognized the similarity in core values and principles, and wondered if that would hold true relative to other Cottage businesses. To test the question I deployed my management team to visit a number of "mom and pop" businesses.

We noted several characteristics that were indeed in line with the kinds of things we tried to achieve under the "high performance organization" banner. Characteristics like valuing each individual, teamwork, expecting each team member to be responsible, facilitating a clear understanding of where the team was going and what was needed from each individual to get there, and a high level of trust. These values weren't universal, but they seemed to cluster in the small businesses that proved successful over time.

I began to realize a significant fact. There is something about human nature that, if paid attention to, actually facilitates positive organizational behavior and results. A man by the name of Douglas McGregor postulated this as Theory X and Theory Y.

McGregor's Theory X is the belief that people are generally lazy and don't want to work. Managers have to watch employees closely and control what they do in order to see results.

Theory Y is the belief that people want to do well. Workers want to make a contribution and be recognized for it. McGregor suggested that individuals who possess the ability to think about and solve organizational problems are broadly distributed through organizations—neither the desire nor the ability is restricted to a few especially skilled individuals.

The more time I spent starting new organizations and evaluating the elements of success, the more I saw the truth of Theory Y. Modern organizations typically designated few queen bees and a lot of worker bees. But I found evidence everywhere that the inherent capability of ordinary people can be tapped to create astounding results.

Ancient Wisdom

One of my favorite examples of this is the story of Nehemiah, the governor who organized the rebuilding of Jerusalem in 432 B.C. For 150 years, every effort to rebuild the ruined city failed until Nehemiah was appointed governor by the Babylonian king Artaxerxes.

What he did was simple and brilliant. The walls of the city had been knocked down and the massive gates reduced to ashes. This allowed their enemies to ransack the city at will. Nehemiah gave the residents of Jerusalem a mission: "Come, let us rebuild the walls and we will no longer be in disgrace!" Certainly this wasn't the first time anyone considered this. What they lacked was an effective plan. Nehemiah had one. His plan was for each family to rebuild the portion of the wall next to their house and for shopkeepers to do the same. He had the priests rebuild the sheep gate—special because that was the gate they primarily used. In other words, he asked people to concentrate on rebuilding where they had a personal stake.

You may be thinking, as I did, "it took 150 years to figure out that?" Then I realized some similarities. Look at industry today. It's been 150 years since the Industrial Revolution began, and many companies still haven't figured "it" out.

Here's the rest of the story. The work to rebuild the walls proceeded smoothly and quickly until about half way. That's when their adversaries saw the plan coming together and moved to disrupt the project. But wise Nehemiah picked up on their plot. He adjusted human resources to increase safety and security, and the work continued.

Then enemies of the work went after Nehemiah and tried to distract him. He was so focused and principle-centered that they couldn't pull him off course. Nothing they tried worked. His course included making sure all issues and disputes were settled quickly and he set a terrific example by freely sharing all he had. As governor he owned quite a bit in the way of resources. *Good to Great* author Jim Collins might say Nehemiah was a true Level 5 Leader.

The end result established a standard we would envy even today. In Nehemiah's own words: "So the wall was completed…in fifty-two days. When all our enemies heard about this, all the surrounding nations were afraid and lost their self confidence…"

Fifty-two days. I'm not sure we could pull permits for a project that size in fifty-two days! Nehemiah proved that breaking work down to family-sized units, plus utilizing a leader who can be trusted to handle peripheral matters, generates extraordinary shared success.

Back to the 20th Century

What Nehemiah learned to be true for workers in his day held true for the twentieth century as well. The next step in my journey, I managed the P&G plant in Euskirchen, Germany. The plant was up and running and it was time to figure out how to improve efficiency. Efficiency is a calculation of the amount of good end product as a percentage of the total amount possible. Downtime, equipment slowdowns and bad quality all reduce the efficiency percentage. Several years after Procter & Gamble essentially invented disposable diaper-making technology, efficiency levels were still stuck in the seventy percent range.

At Euskirchen I found the better of two worlds: American creativity (ready, fire, aim) and the German penchant for precision (tick, tick, tick). I saw this as an opportunity to marry the two—combining the detailed refinement of every process (German engineering) with highly involved teams (the Cottage) to improve efficiency. We planned a campaign to improve efficiency to over ninety percent.

Disposable diapers are made on long machines that pull in component materials on one end and push diapers out the other end, at a rate of something over five hundred per minute; over eight diapers every second at full speed.

We had 26 machines manufacturing diapers in a variety of sizes. We wanted to start with a win right up front so, rather than take on the entire facility, we turned the project over to the department producing the smallest and easiest product to manufacture.

The German teams reasoned that stopping and starting the equipment was the primary source of bad quality as well as lost production. After a thorough analysis, they delivered a

Paraeto chart that clearly identified every problem capable of causing the machine to stop, from most common to least.

So far, so good. Then German precision kicked in with intense focus on one thing. I've seen that degree of focus so rarely in American industry. When was the last time you really focused on just one thing or saw anyone else do it? Through analysis, the Germans identified the problem causing the most stoppage, and fixed it. I mean, they fixed it—forever! They didn't do it overnight and it took several prototypes, but when they were done, the problem was permanently solved.

Then they moved to the second problem and fixed that. Then the third, and so it went until they had engineered out all the inefficiency they could. At this point the department was operating at 94% efficiency versus 75% when they started.

You may ask why they hadn't already done this. The reason is simple and common in industry. They hadn't been asked! German society is like ours in that it is normal for a few bosses to do all the thinking and directing while most workers just do what they are told—even when they know better. What we did was open the problem up to the workers. We got them involved, and they responded. It was the same strategy Nehemiah employed when he said to each family, "Repair the wall next to your own house."

That was just the beginning. The other departments watched what happened and took the initiative to schedule their own upgrades. So the process continued until the entire plant operated at over ninety percent efficiency. We became a model in the company, and a regular stop on the P&G management tour.

Cross Cultural Dynamics
We were to begin producing an adult diaper in Germany and there happened to be a surplus machine at our plant in Greenville, North Carolina. We hired a mechanical contractor

in North Carolina to dismantle the machine and install it at our plant in Germany.

We prepared one side of a manufacturing area for the installation, separating it from the rest of the plant with an expanse of ceiling-to-floor curtain.

We took delivery of the equipment and the mechanical contractor's craftspeople arrived right behind it. These were some "good ol' boys" from the Carolinas. They arrived on a Saturday with the idea that they would have Sunday to get over jet lag and be ready to go Monday morning. Sunday came and sometime around midday, they decided to sample some fine German beer. No doubt a couple of them had spent a tour in Germany courtesy of the U.S. government, and I don't think it took much convincing to get their colleagues to join them at the local hofbrauhaus.

I can also imagine that these good ol' boys, used to domestic brews back home, found the local beer outstanding, especially with a few bratwursts. And, apparently, they enjoyed themselves—immensely.

Monday morning came, and the Carolina boys were in bad shape. Fortunately, the first person they encountered at the plant was our safety manager, Manfred Ehrmann, who quickly sized up the situation and sent them back to the hotel to sleep it off. They returned on Tuesday, refreshed, embarrassed, and ready to work.

I was out of town that Tuesday and Wednesday, but on Thursday I was back and wanted to tour the construction area. It just so happened that I went with our safety manager, Manfred, who filled me in on Monday's false start. As we approached the curtain separating the construction area, the plant displayed its typical orderly appearance and hummed with productivity. Stepping through the curtain, I was suddenly in redneck country. Fifteen workers plying their craft with hard hats on backward, a variety of denim overalls and shirts, cheeks stuffed with whatever it is those fellows stick between their cheek and gum.

The workers seemed a bit on edge. Manfred noticed it as well and said, "Look, they're nervous because I'm the one who sent them home on Monday and they know that you're the boss. Perhaps they're wondering if you're going to do something more to them."

As he said this I realized that they had no idea I was an American. I do have enough German blood to look the part. I decided to have a little fun. I walked up behind two of the men and stood, just a little too close, for moment, looking over their shoulders. Then I said in my best southern drawl, "Ah heer y'all fum Nawth Ca'lina. How y'all doin?"

They both jumped up and turned around and one of them said, "Yassuh, whar y'all fum?" I explained to them who I was and what I was doing there. We shot the breeze about German beer, bratwurst, and North Carolina barbecue, and they seemed to relax into the conversation. That was good; I didn't want their time in Germany to continue down the unpleasant path they had started off on—for their sake and mine.

About that same time, two executives came to see me from corporate headquarters. I was aware that my tenure in Germany was about up and my boss had alerted me that this was more than a plant tour. They were coming to talk about my next assignment. I was excited and nervous. Excited because I had done well in Germany and expected to be rewarded with a bigger challenge; nervous because I didn't have a clue what was in store for me.

Chapter 6

The Case Study

❧ ❧

It was a Sunday afternoon when I talked about my next assignment with the P&G executives from the U.S. We weren't far into the meeting when they made the proposition. "John, we'd like you to move to Perry, Florida and manage the Foley pulp mill."

This mill ranked dead last on my list of possible locations. In fact, many in Procter and Gamble figured it was the end of the line. I swallowed hard and tried to maintain my composure, but this proposition made me feel unappreciated and devalued. I had done a pretty good job managing this huge German plant; how could they push me out to a stinky pulp mill?

They went on to describe the "opportunity." Code word to mean "big problem." The business at Foley was struggling and needed someone to lead a transition from its outdated, stuck in the mud, traditional ways to something more in keeping with the current pace of business. It needed to transform to a "high performance" system, employing modern approaches to get everyone in the organization involved and contributing to their full potential. I had no experience with anything like this turnaround effort.

I wasn't about to be won over by their "opportunity," and my response was pretty negative. "Thanks for your interest in me and the offer of this opportunity but I don't think I'd be interested, what else do you have?" Thanks, but no thanks!

To their credit they didn't take my negative attitude at face value. They just said, "Well, why don't you talk it over with your wife tonight, and we can talk more tomorrow."

That was fine with me—I needed to slink away and lick my wounds anyway. Kathie would be sympathetic; she wouldn't like the sound of this any more than I did.

As I drove to the house I continued to fuss and fume about how unappreciative they and the company were considering all I'd done for them. Didn't they know what I brought to the table? Maybe now was the time to just walk away; go to work for someone who would appreciate my talents and abilities. Maybe it was time to start my own business.

Kathie was waiting for me, eager to hear all about the proposal. To Kathie "all about it" meant every detail, from the décor of the room where we met to what each man wore. I was rarely in the mood to provide that much detail, and even less so this time. I went right to the bottom line: "They want us to go to Foley, that stinky old pulp mill in Florida." If you've ever smelled a pulp mill, you know I wasn't exaggerating, but in this case, the prospect stunk just as much as the plant itself!

I expected Kathie to join me in the indignity of it all but she didn't even blink; she just replied, "Well, what did you tell them?"

I didn't want to answer directly until I made sure Kathie understood how wrong they were to even suggest the assignment. So I carried on about what an insult it was until she seized a pause in my rant to ask once more, "Okay, so what did you tell them?"

"I told them the only thing I could tell them—I told them they could go pound salt and take this job with them!" An exaggeration I know, but I felt emphasis was needed. Kathie was being much too cool in the middle of this terrible situation.

She replied, "Don't you think you should at least consider it?" I couldn't believe my ears! My own wife had turned against me. But as we talked about it I began to settle down, and gradually saw she was right. I was letting my ego get in the way of simply considering the offer of a new assignment. No one had a gun to my head. There had been no suggestion that this was the only possibility. It was just the first assignment the company asked me to consider. Now it was up to me to respond.

I determined to be a little calmer about the whole matter, but I tossed and turned in bed that night as I stewed about that stinky pulp mill.

We met again the next day and, though I didn't say no, I pretty well indicated that I wasn't interested. Finally, one of them said, "Look, why don't you and Kathie take a trip over there and scout it out. Take a close look before you make up your mind."

I told them it would probably be a waste of money, but if they were willing to foot the bill then I'd be happy to take advantage of the trip.

Less than a month later we drove south on U.S. 19 toward Perry, Florida. Unlike my first trip to Mehoopany, Pennsylvania, I had done a little research about the Perry area.

"Isn't it amazing," I commented to Kathie, "the one location I didn't want anything to do with is the very place the company wants us to go."

"It won't be as bad as you're thinking," Kathie replied. "Maybe we'll find it to be just great."

"I doubt it. I've heard a lot about this place, and it's no cup of tea. Over the years it's been a pretty rough and tumble area. Word on the street is that the area was originally settled by people escaping southern prisons back in the 1800s, and just a few years ago the FBI cracked one of the biggest drug operations in the country right there."

"Maybe all that has changed now," Kathie suggested. "Let's not judge it 'til we see it, I think it will be fine." That kind of thinking was the farthest thing from my mind - I wasn't done being indignant. If it weren't for Kathie's patience and encouragement, I would have never considered the prospect of working there.

As we approached Perry the terrain became flatter and flatter. Mile after mile of dense jungle-like foliage on either sides of the road.

Occasionally we spotted stands of farmed pine trees at different stages of growth, from just-planted seedlings to tall, mature trees. Farther from the highway we saw the boundaries of the tree farm were made irregular by swampy patches of cypress and hardwood trees. "Oh no," I thought. "They're trying to sell me the proverbial Florida swampland!"

I wondered if this was part of the land base for the Foley pulp mill. It actually didn't look that bad; apparently half of it was just too wet to be used for anything. I suspected the place must have been teeming with wildlife. It occurred to me that growing pine for the pulp industry was probably a very good use for this land. That would be a valuable benefit of having a large pulp mill being located in the area. For the first time I had a slightly positive feeling toward the situation.

As we reached the margin of town we found a strip of gas stations and fast food joints typical of most small American towns. I decided I needed a break, so we ducked into a Wendy's restaurant. A burger and fries improved my mood some more and we drove to the other end of the strip to find the 50s vintage Howard Johnson motel where we were scheduled to stay.

"Hello, my name is John Sipple. Do you have a reservation for me?" I said, fully expecting that they did. I was wrong. I returned to the car exclaiming, "Guess what, no reservation! I think this is a sign; we're not supposed to be here!"

Kathie allowed that might be possible but encouraged me to check the other motels in the area. We did and, of course, they didn't have a reservation for us either. So, we went back to Ho Jo's, and I asked to use the phone. I was a bit hot by this point, and I don't mean from Florida's steamy weather.

I called the current plant manager who was very apologetic about the reservation and confirmed that Ho Jo's was indeed the best lodging in town. He also said that a fellow by the name of Dick Heydt would come by in about an hour to take us on a tour of the community. At that moment I had seen all of this place I wanted to see but agreed and hung up the phone.

From the moment we met Dick things began to improve. Dick Heydt is the kind of person folks can't help but like. He was obviously a real professional, but he was also warm and very interested in us—something I needed a little of at that point.

We spent a little time just talking before Dick gave us the tour. The town was fairly typical of small southern towns— radiating out from a central courthouse and a cluster of churches. The houses, mostly built during the '30s, '40s, and '50s, were neat with only a few in need of paint.

We saved the pulp mill till last. I have to say I was impressed by the sheer immensity. It was about the biggest manufacturing facility I had ever seen and to think I might soon be responsible for it was a little disconcerting. I started pumping Dick for more information about the place.

"It's been pretty rough here the past few years," Dick explained. "The business did fairly well throughout the seventies, but we've been on a downhill slide since then."

"Why?" I asked.

"It seems to be a combination of things," Dick replied. "First of all, we've got quite a morale problem. The hourly workers don't respect or get along with management at all, and there are too many breakdowns. Our technical reliability is getting worse year by year, and we can't seem to get any money or support to do anything about it."

Great. Just as I thought. This place was going nowhere fast! I asked Dick what he thought it would take to turn things around. He said the primary need was for the organization to have a solid sense of direction—a direction they could support. He also expressed a need for corporate support to repair what needed fixed. Bricks fell from the walls, ceilings were in danger of falling in, and there were dangerously corroded pipes.

I appreciated Dick's forthrightness. He didn't duck tough questions, and I believed his analysis was probably accurate. Further, though the picture he painted was not pretty, I had the sense that if we remedied the problems, *maybe* the situation could be turned around.

Kathie and I spent the next couple of days looking at houses and learning more about the community. Before making the trip Kathie had made a list of the things that were important if we were to make the move—things like schools, churches, and shopping.

Our oldest daughter, Kim, was about to finish high school in Germany and didn't want to move back to the U.S. and then immediately go off to college. So we were interested to know if she could enroll in college and still live at home for a year or so. It turned out there was a junior college within driving distance that had a good record of helping young people making the transition from high school to university.

Everything on Kathie's list fell into place including one rather unusual item—at least I thought it was unusual. High on her list was that she would see no snakes, a condition she regarded as neither unusual nor unreasonable. Can you imagine even considering that we could live in small town Florida and not see a snake? I humored her. But she didn't see any snakes on our visit so she checked that off the list. When we moved away from Perry nine years later Kathie still had not seen a snake. So, there you have it.

On that first trip to Perry, I verified that the stories I'd heard were essentially true, though somewhat exaggerated. The area did have traits no one could be proud of. But I began to notice something else. The people were warm and friendly. Even those who initially looked a little rough and standoffish were plenty friendly if I took the time to talk to them. And there was something else. There was no pretense of being something they weren't. Their demeanor reflected their unspoken motto, which I found refreshing. "What you see is what you get."

On the last day of our visit I toured the pulp mill with Dick. Nothing had been said to the organization about the possibility of my coming as the new plant manager so I was introduced as a customer, which was true. One of the pulp products made here was shipped to the plant I managed in Germany to be used as absorbent core material in the disposable diapers we produced.

If the place was big from the outside, it seemed massive inside. I had never been around technology like this. It just about blew my mind. I spent my career in attractive, well-maintained facilities that manufactured P&G's line of consumer products. I wasn't used to the messy and out-of-control appearance of this facility.

The last place Dick took me was the top of the mill's biggest recovery boiler—an enormous, nine-story unit that burns the lignin that is removed during pulping. The boiler recovers a portion of the by-product that can be returned as "cooking liquor" for processing future batches of wood chips.

The view was impressive; after all, this was the highest point in the county. As I gazed over the mill itself I couldn't help but notice its ugliness. Then I rehearsed all the problems of coming to work here. But for some reason I felt strangely challenged by it all.

I suppose it was a little like the scene in the movie Patton where George C. Scott, in the role of Patton, gazes over a battlefield and said: "God, I love it!" I don't mean to say I love war, but at that moment on top of the recovery boiler I had the same kind of feeling about that place and the people in it: "God, I love it!" Even with the problems, I loved the challenge, the responsibility, and most of all, the people.

We left town that evening, beginning the journey back to Germany and our children. I didn't have to tell the company about my decision for a couple of weeks but both Kathie and I knew that we had our marching orders; we would be back.

Chapter 7

Searching for a Strategy

A few months later we arrived in Perry, Florida to dive into this new "opportunity." The business had deteriorated badly, and seemed near total collapse. The workers were very bitter toward the company and its leaders and, frankly, the place felt out of control. But I found people with a great deal of technical skill—testimony to better years.

I was overwhelmed by the magnitude of the problem. I had no experience with "smokestack" industry, either in terms of specific technologies or management approaches. I had no coherent idea how to even approach the beast.

One thing was clear; whatever strategy we chose required rapid implementation. There was no time for extensive research and analysis—though we had to do a little just to figure out where to begin.

I discussed all of this early on with Ken Stuparyk. Ken was a Canadian, recently transferred from our plant in Grande Prairie, Alberta. He had experienced more advanced approaches to management and had been brought in as part of the effort to improve performance at Foley.

I instantly liked Ken. He operated in high gear all the time but had enough sensitivity to stop and listen to a good idea or concern. Ken lamented the overall resistance to change in the organization—a problem made worse by a ban on hiring. He felt totally stymied in his efforts.

I asked Ken what his approach had been up to that point. They had organized project teams with people from across the organization, including managers and hourly workers.

"What do these cross-organizational teams do?" I asked.

"Well, one of them is working on communications," Ken answered. "Another is studying organizational structures, and a third has been working on pay and progression ideas to provide more incentive for the workforce."

Guessing that this wasn't all that was going on, I asked Ken to tell me what else they had tried to accomplish in addition to making a little pulp. He outlined several more initiatives, including a group trying to figure out how to improve technical reliability and another working on a new computerized control system to replace the old manual systems that had existed for years.

It seemed to me the organization's leaders didn't really know what to do, so they were trying everything, hoping for a breakthrough. While this may have seemed like a smart way to tackle the difficulties, it put such a drain on resources that it only aggravated the problem. The people saw this as more crazy stuff from "management" which caused them to become more and more cynical and the business results grew steadily worse.

There was no doubt this was the most difficult situation I had ever encountered. P&G was just beginning the transition of older, "traditional" work systems to "high involvement" and "high performance" systems, which allowed for much more involvement of the people in the direction and decisions for the daily operation, and consequently higher performance. We knew a lot about how to accomplish these things in new facilities and organizations but we hadn't hit on a formula for transforming existing, traditional systems.

I recalled my own struggle when I was first asked to consider the job at Foley, and the events leading to my decision. I had done a complete about-face regarding the opportunity here, and my mission had become clear. The immediate problem was that there was no clarity about how to accomplish the mission.

But maybe I did know how to do it. Over years of working with a variety of organizations I had learned how to move toward an objective by involving rather than directing people. The more I worked this way, the more it fell into a fairly predictable approach with reasonably predictable results. My new situation was very different, but that didn't mean the philosophy wouldn't work just as well.

I also considered my roots in the Cottage business and the values I learned there. I remembered the lesson I learned making the jewelry box for my sister, and my father's admonishment that if it was worth doing it was worth doing right. It had become crystal clear that these values played a significant role in all my efforts to involve people in organizational change.

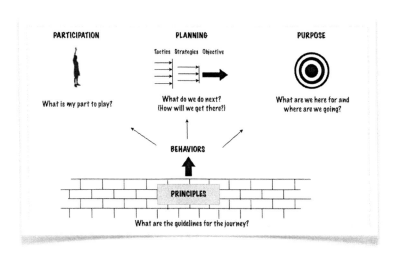

The Four P's

I began sketching out a simple diagram to show Ken what I had in mind (see diagram above). In the upper right hand corner I wrote the word PURPOSE, and below it sketched concentric circles to look like a target. I wrote the questions, "What are we here for and where are we going?" I explained my conviction that these are the first questions people in any organization ask, and it's up to the leaders to answer them. After all, why should we expect people to be excited about going to an unknown place?

I said our answer had to include more than the destination: it must paint a picture of what the destination would look like when we got there, with enough detail for individuals to envision themselves in the picture and decide if they wanted to make the journey.

"Once people know where they are going, what is their next question?" I asked Ken.

He responded quickly, "Oh, that's easy; they'll want to know how to get there and what to do next."

"That's what I would want to know," I agreed and to the left of the word **PURPOSE** I wrote the word **PLANNING** and sketched out several arrows in the general shape of a rocket ship. I labeled the lead arrow "objective," the next group of arrows "strategies," and the final group "tactics."

From what Ken described earlier it was clear they were working on several tactics but lacked a clear understanding of where it all led. Once people understood the ultimate purpose and the primary objective toward achieving that purpose, then an orderly plan could be developed to focus effort and create synergy.

With clear understanding of the overall purpose and short-term objective it would also be possible to determine which strategies and tactics would propel them forward and which would create drag. Knowing what not to do is as important as knowing what to do.

Moving left across the page, the next word on my diagram was **PARTICIPATION**. Below it I drew a stick figure person and said, "Once we know where we're going and what to tackle first, there is a logical question to ask next."

Ken hesitated. "I'm not sure what you mean."

"Imagine yourself as a member of the organization," I said. "We've done some things to help you picture where we are going, and you like what you see. And we've worked on developing a plan to give you a clear understanding of how we will make the journey. At this point, what would you need to know?"

Ken thought for a moment, "I guess it would be like getting involved in a sport of some sort. Once I determined what it was all about and knew I'd like to get involved, my question would be something like 'What's my position? What position do I play?'"

"You've got it."

"But what if some don't really want to play?" Ken ventured. "I can't imagine everyone just jumping on the bandwagon!"

"True," I admitted. "And we have to answer the question for them even if they aren't asking it yet. Giving them a part to play can go a long way in connecting their hearts and minds to the overall effort."

"Ken, there's one more part to this picture, and it may be the most important part of all." I wrote the word **PRINCIPLES** below the rest of the diagram and around the word sketched what looked like a wall or a foundation. Above the word **PRINCIPLES** I wrote the word **BEHAVIOR** and drew an arrow connecting the two words.

As I sketched, I explained that **PRINCIPLES** are the shared values and beliefs of an organization, and they determine the overall character or **BEHAVIOR** of that organization. "For example, if there is a shared value or principle that says 'In order to be successful we must support each other' then that should result in the behavior of people working together more effectively than an organization that does not embrace that principle."

Ken said, "I guess the question that goes with this one is, 'What are the guidelines for the journey?'"

"That's a great way to think about it. Principles act as guidelines for behavior in the organization. In effect, they function as a kind of foundation."

I went on to describe how important it is for leaders to model the principles and behaviors. "If the leaders do this consistently, people will begin to follow their lead, and soon the entire organization will behave in similar fashion. Leaders who 'walk the talk' are leaders people are more apt to follow."

Ken was getting excited now. "And if by leaders you mean all leaders—managers, union officials, natural leaders in the organization—then this really becomes powerful. I can see where nearly everyone would want to get on board."

"Exactly. All the leaders you mentioned have the ability to lead and they will lead one way or another. Best we try to get them all on the same page."

As we talked through this approach and assessed where the Foley organization stood, three issues became clear. First, although some effort had been made to clarify the organization's purpose, much more was needed. The purpose simply wasn't clear to folks. Second, there was a pretty decent set of principle statements, but they were irrelevant to the purposes of the company since they were largely ignored. Third, the action plan needed a much sharper strategic focus. There were too many things on the plate to give anything proper attention, and quite a few things got no attention at all.

The organization viewed current management efforts as just one more trip around the block that would yield no more than the prior one (or the one before that). In those first days at Foley I often heard, "We were here before you came and we'll be here when you leave and nothing much will have changed." The organization was understandably apathetic and unmotivated to participate beyond, "Just tell me what to do, and I'll do it." Left unsaid, but obviously implied: "But don't expect me to think about how to do it better."

As we discussed how to implement the model we sketched out, Ken said, "I see now that I've been making a bad situation worse. The business is running poorly, and I've been trying to get the management team to accept several new initiatives at once. I'd be lucky to get them to accept even one!"

"Ken, let's say that our primary objective is to get this business out of the ditch and on the road to success. What key strategy would we pick first to make that happen?"

"There would have to be something about technical reliability. And our process isn't producing good quality. Then there are the environmental issues. And of course the awful trust issue between the workers and management gets in the way of everything!"

That's how Ken and I began our campaign to get Foley out of the ditch and rolling forward. What we really wanted was one solid strategy to overcome inertia and leverage everything else that was stuck. We worked on this at some length with the rest of the leadership team. I imagine our desire to find that "one thing" sounded like a pipedream to them. But I was unwilling to give up the quest. I figured the organization was so unstable that, at best, we might pull off one thing in addition to running the base business, poor as it was. Because the situation was so tenuous, we had to be right about that one thing—I wasn't counting on a second chance.

With perseverance, an idea began to emerge! We would stop all the teams previously formed and constitute just one new team of representatives from across the organization—all invited to help determine the strategy. Of course, it wouldn't be much of a team to begin with. We would have to develop that in real time and then, together, identify and tackle the *one thing* that could move us forward.

Chapter 8

Design Team

O ver the years the people at Foley had been used to a certain style of leadership, which could best be described
as directive and "top down." Bosses decided and workers
executed (more or less). People had no ownership in what
went on, they did the minimum required to assure they'd get
their paycheck each Thursday. Back in the day, the original
bosses knew how to run the operation, but they gradually left
for other assignments or retired, leaving less accomplished
replacements to manage the ever-more-experienced workforce. This is a formula for disaster in most workplaces.

At Foley, some effort had been expended to smoothen
management transitions, but always in the old "top down"
style. No buy-in from the organization was ever achieved.
Over the years, performance decayed incrementally, matched
by a growing cynicism that anything dreamed up by management could never be right.

Assembling a cross-organizational team to play a serious
role in determining the future of this major (and majorly
underperforming) business unit was (to say the least) a challenge. This was the only hope we saw for creating a setting
where all parties could have meaningful input into the future

of the business. In that respect it was a legitimate attempt to develop a kind of Cottage setting—a small, team-oriented workgroup within a large organization. If it worked it might be possible to replicate the model across the whole organization. But if it failed, it could spell the end for the business unit.

There was absolutely no assurance it would work. The workers were fed up, the union representatives were generally averse to anything that interrupted the familiar routine, and the salaried managers had very little experience (or interest) in relinquishing one bit of their direction-setting authority.

For the moment, however, I had the upper hand. I was the plant manager and I was perfectly clear about the mission. I hadn't been told how to do it—I don't believe anyone knew—but I had the support of the corporation, at least for now. If we didn't demonstrate progress within the first year I'd likely lose that support, so I needed to forge ahead—fast!

Ken began developing a process to form the new group. With about 1200 employees, we determined it would take around 35 to achieve effective representation across the entire site, including a woodlands group, finance and accounting, systems, engineering, and the plant operations where the majority of our people worked. We intended to allow each working unit to determine whom to send as their representative.

We hit a snag right out of the gate. Almost no one volunteered. I knew there was reluctance to get involved in anything outside the norm, but I had no idea it would be this difficult.

Ken brought me the news. "John, I really don't know what to do at this point. Everything I understand about developing participative work systems says that you must start with people who are interested. We don't have many. The few who have volunteered are probably doing it just to

79

get out of work." I suspected he was right; it was August in Florida when pulp mills are most unpleasant.

The more we discussed the problem the more we realized there were no good choices. We would have to assign people to this project, knowing if we couldn't get them excited about a better future for Foley, our chances would be slim with the rest of the organization.

We accepted the handful of volunteers, and conscripted the rest. I remember my first meeting with them. You could have cut the tension with a knife. Most took a "wait and see" approach. And who could blame them? I imagine most of them were thinking, "This too shall pass, then we'll get back to our normal routine."

But not everyone. A few members in the group were actually quite interested—managers mostly, like Dick Heydt, but also a couple of hourly workers who were clearly going against the grain of their peers. At this early stage, the fact that these positive people were involved only added to the overall tension.

We forged ahead, running the group through a battery of training exercises to educate them on the principles and concepts of "participative work systems." If we could help them see how we intended to involve every member of the organization in the daily responsibilities of the business, we would achieve our aim.

One exercise was to accomplish a task as a team. The results were mixed. Most everyone appeared to enjoy the process but when asked if they thought such an approach could be replicated throughout the organization they were nearly unanimous in their opinion that it could not. Nonetheless, we felt a small measure of success. This group of reluctant draftees had actually enjoyed the training. It was a start.

Next we divided the group of 35 into traveling parties and sent them to observe the work systems at half a dozen Procter and Gamble locations. These operations were up and running with the participative characteristics we wanted to implement at Foley.

I traveled with the union executive committee to the P&G paper plant in Mehoopany, Pennsylvania where I cut my teeth as a young shift manager. I counted on the Mehoopany plant to demonstrate just how perfect these participative systems really were.

We scheduled three days to observe the total operation at the Mehoopany site—including the mix of communications and meeting approaches used to ensure that everyone received the information they needed to do their work. Participative work systems make much more information available to each person than top-down systems. The idea is that if workers have the same kind of information as owners, they will be able to solve problems and make decisions that enhance the productivity of the entire organization. If this were a "need to know" system, our view was that every worker was on a need-to-know level.

In the beginning we hit a small snag. Our visit was set up in a highly structured fashion and Freddie Rogers, the union president at Foley, wasn't convinced he would see things as they really were. Freddie wanted the freedom to wander around, night or day, and view the operation without restriction. He figured if he viewed the plant without prior notice he'd get the real scoop. The leadership at the Mehoopany site wasn't about to agree to that arrangement, but I could understand Freddie's position. We worked out a compromise so the executive committee could view the operation with a guide other than me (which I think was the real issue).

George Harvey, a union vice president, was assigned to stick close to me throughout the trip, to pick my brain and find out what the new guy was all about.

George should have been a lawyer. He was very good at formulating questions to get the most out of conversations. I answered everything as truthfully and openly as I knew how.

I knew George and the rest of this executive committee were very important—perhaps the key element—to achieving the transition we needed to undergo as an organization. The only way to get them to trust me was to be completely open and honest with them and hope they would pick up on my sincere desire to help everyone in our business succeed.

It must be said that companies too often use participation concepts at the expense of workers. Workers are invited to become more involved and more productive only to find themselves or their colleagues laid-off as an unintended consequence. While it is true that high performance concepts can lead to greater productivity and a need for fewer employees, there are very good ways and very poor ways to handle this quandary.

Some general managers are so shortsighted that, once better efficiency kicks in they want to let go of any unnecessary workers, seeing them as dead weight. They don't take into consideration what these layoffs will do to morale and momentum (not the mention what it does to laid-off workers). In most cases, the number of employees can be reduced simply by not hiring to replace normal attrition. It's not as fast, but this approach gets an organization to the same place with higher morale and momentum for continuing progress, not to mention gaining better reputations in the communities.

The real money in a participative work system doesn't come from trimming the work force. What makes the cash register ring is improving the overall process to reach new levels of reliability and productivity. This can only happen with a committed and involved organization. The effort should lead to improved product quality and lower cost, facilitating increased sales and growth. If the whole system is harmonized, it's possible for the gains in productivity to produce business growth that requires the additional capacity of those extra workers.

This brings me back to George Harvey and his effort to figure me out. I guessed that he was concerned about just where this participation idea would lead, so I did my best to be up front about how many employees might or might not be required in the future. It wasn't possible for me to make any guarantees—I wasn't at all sure where our efforts might lead at that point. But I communicated my genuine concern for each person in the organization and explained that I didn't intend for this effort to wind up getting people dumped.

I was aware that unions often viewed these types of systems initiatives as union busting techniques, so I tried to alleviate that concern before the question was even asked. My basic message to George during that trip—and to all the executive committee throughout the transition—was that I believed we needed each other to fulfill our objectives. I reasoned—it's a shared objective: to assure future success for the business and for each individual in the business. In fact, success for each individual is dependent on the success of the overall business.

As the site visit proceeded I grew concerned about what the executive committee witnessed. I hoped the Mehoopany site would be at its best and the committee would be overwhelmed at the wonderful things they observed. I noted several things that weren't working the way I hoped. In one team meeting we observed, the local technicians complained about their manager, who was not there and had apparently forgotten to do something he promised.

My thoughts ranged from "how awful this is going" to "I need to report this to the plant manager" to "how dare they air their dirty laundry in front of guests!" The Mehoopany technicians concluded their complaint by saying they would schedule a short meeting with the manager later that day to resolve the issue. The importance of that didn't register with me until later.

I managed to get Freddie Rogers aside that afternoon to ask him what he thought of the visit and, hopefully, assure him that the meeting that morning was "abnormal" as far as I was concerned.

Freddie said, "So far the visit has been just great, and I really appreciate the opportunity to take a look at another workplace." Then he said, "You know, I never did really believe these high performance systems were as perfect as y'all make them out to be…"

I'm thinking, oh no, we really messed up by bringing them here.

"…And, what we've seen here isn't perfect by any means."

Inside I'm groaning - but still listening.

"Take that meeting this morning for example…"

Here it comes!

"…Those folks had a problem with their manager and it really wasn't much different than a group in our place might have with their manager…"

How am I ever going to set this right?

"…But, when they said they were going to schedule a time to resolve the issue that really impressed me. You know, that never happens at Foley. People there just accept the way things are and never do anything to make them better!"

You could have knocked me over with a feather. My thoughts had carried me down the wrong path altogether! I immediately saw several important points that continue to influence my thinking today.

First, trying to convince someone that something they've not seen is perfect is a waste of time because it's not believable. Second, trusting the inherent wisdom of people to recognize a better way when they see it is better than blustering and browbeating. Third, and most profound to me, **average workers are not looking for Utopia in the work place;**

they know better. What they want is to have a say in what goes on there—to help make the workplace better.

Back at Foley, we took time to debrief and process what each group observed. We encouraged each person to discuss what thoughts came to them as a result of visiting another workplace. There was one overarching theme. Nearly everyone was impressed that people just like them had so much opportunity to be involved in setting the direction of their respective operating units.

Like Freddie, they all saw what they perceived as flaws in the work systems they visited. But the result of this turned out to be very positive. Their attitudes turned from not wanting to be involved in any way to an eagerness to design a system that would include the best of what they had seen and eliminate the flaws they'd spotted. In short, they looked forward to designing their own work system, a system that would uniquely fit their culture and technology.

It appeared that our group of non-volunteers was rapidly being transformed into a team. They were beginning to develop the kind of "ownership" attitude I remembered folks having in the Cottage industry of my youth, and anyplace where there was an honest invitation to complete participation.

It seems we located a key strategy for unlocking the organizational logjam—a new work system design to facilitate everyone's involvement and contribution. From a business point of view it made sense. True, we had other needs, like improving our technical reliability, but we needed organizational alignment to generate the capacity to handle the other needs. We were ready to move forward and it was obvious we'd struck a chord in the hearts and minds of the first 35 individuals. We'd found our *one thing*.

Chapter 9

The Design

࿔ ࿔

Principles and Purpose

Armed with our training experience and site visits, the design team was ready to tackle the work we had been chartered to do. We began with a thorough assessment of our status. This took some time and produced a few spirited exchanges but for the most part there was pretty close agreement regarding the present standing at Foley.

We shifted our focus to the future. Comparing what we saw on the site visits with the assessment of our current situation gave us a starting point to discuss what we wanted our business to look like in the future. We needed one more thing; we needed to know the guiding principles for our journey together.

Our challenge was not how to develop a list of guiding principles—someone now long gone had previously developed a set of principles. The question was whether they were the right principles and, if so, how to execute them. The organization in general, and the design team specifically, were not of one mind about that.

<u>Our starting principles included:</u>

1. Leadership is the responsibility of all employees.
2. Things happen best when we work together.
3. Every employee is an owner.
4. Do the best you can; strive for excellence.
5. Achieve and maintain balance.
6. Flexibility is vital to our changing environment.
7. We care for each other and demonstrate mutual support and respect.
8. Personal honesty and integrity are reflected in all of our actions.
9. Every member is encouraged and allowed to contribute to the business and shares in the personal satisfaction and rewards that come from this.
10. You make the difference.

We had great debate about each one of the statements. Some wanted to start over totally; some wanted to "word-smith" a little and move on; still others wanted to leave the list as we found it and concentrate on implementation. Finally, someone said, "You know, we will never agree to the exact wording, but the spirit of what we want seems to be here!"

That launched another discussion, from which we finally received closure. We decided to leave the statement of principles alone and concentrate on walking the talk instead of just posting the list on a wall or hiding it in a file cabinet.

From this point we began working to define what we wanted the future to look like—focusing our vision. Everything up to this point became raw material for that conversation. We had input from the corporation regarding boundaries (these were broadly stated and not confining in any way). We had a fair grasp of our past and current situation and captured the key elements we wanted to hang on to and those we wanted to change. We had the information from our site visits, and last but not least, we had agreement about the guiding principles to live by.

We organized all of these experiences, observations, principles, relationships concepts, thoughts, and ideas into a fairly lengthy vision statement. Over the years, I've found vision statements are most useful and meaningful for those involved in their development. That proved true in this case. This vision painted a word picture of who we were, where we were going, what we were striving for and what life could be like at Foley. When it was complete, they liked it; they liked it a lot!

Here are some excerpts:

- We...have a dream. We see a total business system... from pine seeds to high value products.
- We see a network of teams functioning with all the skills and knowledge to handle their part of the business.
- Every member of our business feels personally valued, we see real meaning in our work, and we see our ideas becoming reality.
- Our plant is modern and like new, even though portions are nearly 50 years old.
- The plant is quiet and odor free.
- Damage has been eliminated.
- We can tune in to our customers' operations at any time to check how last week's production is doing in their process.
- Our business results are "world class."
- A key ingredient in our success is high quality business plans, which are developed by a cross-section of employees and are deployed to all people.
- The most exciting thing that's happened was when the President awarded us "the prize." That made all of the work of the past 10 years worth it.

In the Cottage of my youth everyone understood where the business was going — after all they were part of the family or might as well have been. This closeness led to a strong sense of belonging, which in turn led to a strong sense of commitment. Completing our vision statement for the future began a process that produced the same effect for the people of Foley.

The leaders of the organization began to consistently walk the talk outlined in our list of principles. We made extensive use of the vision statement to assure understanding and alignment on where we were going. Consequently, we found the organization coming more and more on board. It was not instantaneous; it took time and consistent behavior from the leaders. But it worked and, sooner than you might think, the organization was aligned with our new vision, which left us with a burning question, "how are we going to execute all this?"

Developing the Design

The vision created a broad picture of our future, but where should we begin to execute? Should we concentrate on developing the product and markets? Or, should we go after improving the technology (which certainly needed work)? And what about the organization — our people? All of it required speedy attention but we quickly saw that Job One was providing the organization with the approaches, skills, and systems needed to make the rest of it happen. We needed all 1,200 individuals fully involved in pulling and pushing this wagon where we wanted it to go.

Analyzing our situation in the light of our site visits convinced us our job classification system — a throw back to Frederick Taylor's "scientific management" philosophy — was itself a barrier to productivity (see Chapter 4).

Every hourly employee was assigned a job, and the only way he or she could move to another job was if the person currently doing that job moved on. Ultimately, someone had to retire, quit, or die to create any movement in the organization. Each person was assigned a box and there he stayed. There was very little teamwork. How could there be? It was more of a "you mind your business; I'll mind mine" arrangement.

Holding it all together required supervisors, and lots of them. Every crew for each shift throughout the plant had what amounted to a "straw boss" who maintained order and called the shots. They were there to do the thinking, and the workers were there to do what they were told—end of discussion. There were three more levels of supervisors on top of the shift managers, keeping an eye on them and doing the real thinking I suppose.

This is how Taylor's scientific management played out in industry. The result was a system of work that was horribly restrictive, inflexible, and filled with uninvolved workers and disinterested managers. No wonder the practice collapsed under its own weight.

The design team verified what we already suspected; the work design itself must be recast. To do it right we decided to start with a clean sheet of paper as if we were just starting up the business.

It was fantastic! We began by rethinking how the process operated, what needed to happen, and when it needed to happen, without regard for how it had been done before. We weren't ignoring wisdom from the past; we were reconsidering everything from a "total task" point of view. Each work item plan included not only the immediate physical operation to execute the task, but also equipment maintenance, decisions required, reports issued, quality and cost monitoring, safety standards, and all the information required to accomplish the total task.

As we reorganized the work, we named the new collections of tasks "skill blocks." This became the identifier for logical units of work in our new system. We defined skill blocks for operational/process tasks, maintenance tasks, administrative tasks, and leadership tasks. For each skill block we attached an inventory of skills required to do the work along with the training and qualification standards necessary to become "certified" in the skill block.

Certification was important as a way to assure that each person really had the skills to perform the work. If that meant more training time for one person relative to another we agreed that would be acceptable up to a point. If someone couldn't master a new skill block, we would handle that case by case.

At this point we had a new design for our basic work process and it was good—but not good enough. If we left it at that we would have little more than an upgraded version of our old job classification system. It was going to take more than that to elevate us above the competition.

This is where the Cottage shines. The organizations of the Cottage industry are small, family-oriented, and multi-skilled. The principles we agreed to follow affirmed that "things happen best when we work together" and "we care for each other and demonstrate mutual support and respect" and "we see a network of teams functioning with all the skills and knowledge to handle their part of the business."

Why couldn't we organize our skill blocks in such a way as to facilitate teams that would possess all the skills necessary to handle most of what they would encounter on a day-to-day basis? We began to call the concept "the fully functioning team." We returned to the Cottage for this design characteristic.

Developing the concept, we conceived teams with the mix of skill blocks that would enable them to meet most day-to-day challenges in operations, maintenance, administration, and leadership. Each team would be able to cover its own schedule, manage work absences (sick days and vacations) and coordinate safety, training and project work as needed.

The design began to appeal to everyone; it looked quite different from other work systems they had seen. We needed just one or two more elements to make it work.

One was cross-training our workforce. We didn't want a system in which a person only knew one operation. In order to make this fully functioning team concept work, each person needed to learn at least two skill blocks—a few would learn more. Cross-training creates the flexibility necessary for each team member to be integral to the whole team and complete all the tasks we wanted them to accomplish.

The other element had to do with leadership. We didn't want to have one person on the team become the leader because that would merely replicate the straw bosses we already had. Our site visits confirmed that straw boss leadership failed to achieve the kind of teamwork we wanted.

We began to think about the relationship of a sports team and coach. The coach does not play the game, he or she helps the team prepare and then coaches from the sidelines. Team leaders—often more than one—provide on-field direction. These players relay the coach's direction, give direction on their own or a combination of both.

As we worked with this metaphor, I thought about how similar it was to the Cottage businesses where I grew up. My father was the coach. When new people joined the team, Dad interacted with them directly to get them started, then turned them over to an older hand for further development. These older hands were his on-field leaders. He placed total trust in them to accomplish the work and provide exemplary leadership to newcomers.

We developed a similar approach with our teams at Foley in a concept we called "shared leadership." Typically, on any given team there would be an individual responsible for communications, another for safety, a third for quality, and a fourth for training. These weren't fulltime roles; each team leader blended his or her oversight into the daily routine. If a safety, quality, training or communication issue arose the team knew who would provide leadership to resolve it. Additionally, one of these leaders also assumed a role of overall coordination (team leader). This team leader position rotated and normally wasn't necessary as long as the team functioned smoothly—but available if needed to resolve issues.

The roles were not permanent; they rotated among the team members, giving everyone a chance to try their hand. Of course, some handled leadership better than others. The ones who led easily in any area, tended to do it more. If they weren't assigned to a leadership role when a problem surfaced, they acted as backups, creating greater depth in our fully functioning team concept.

Straw boss supervision focused on command and control. This new coaching focus radically changed the role, with a primary responsibility to develop individuals and the team as a unit. This meant developing a training approach for new roles with coaching and mentoring provided by the most accomplished team members.

We found hourly workers would be much more engaged in the full range of work, pursuing our objectives such as: solving problems, making operational decisions, improving procedures and providing leadership. Our existing first level managers would transition to new roles, merging with the next level of management to reduce one level of hierarchy and simplify the system even more.

The final adjustment to make the new design work really well was changing the pay system from a specific dollar amount for each "job" to a "pay for skills" system that supported our vision. We wanted a system in which people stretched themselves to acquire a greater range of skills to support their team's ability to meet our business objectives.

We had redesigned the work into skill blocks to align the work with the skills necessary to do the work. In the pay for skills concept, as more skill blocks were attained, hourly employees could progress through seven pay levels. We built in regular assessments to assure the skills were maintained at the standard required for certification.

This did not mean everyone would move to the top. Each fully functioning team had a predetermined number of skill blocks and, typically, a few individuals were required for each skill block in each shift to provide flexibility for absence, vacation and training. Staying current in more than two or three skill blocks would be difficult, so only the most adept employees would be able to handle more. Thus, the most versatile team members would reach the highest pay levels and, though a strong individual might be held up for a while, the variety of paths to pay progression meant it would not take nearly as long for pay raises as in the old system. Balanced against improved productivity, this would be a win/win.

Now we had the key concepts to facilitate growth toward our vision for the future. We had radically redesigned our work system including how work would be done, the organizational structure for doing it, what leadership would look like, and how the pay system would support it all. We were poised for our return to the Cottage.

From Concept to Reality

We had a concept—a pretty good idea of what we intended to do and where we intended to go. It was time to translate the concept into reality. We determined four requirements for moving forward:

First, we needed to build out the framework we had for each skill block. We needed detail in terms of the specific competencies required, the approaches and systems we would use to train and develop these abilities, and the standards to which they would be certified. And we needed to reach a final determination on the number of skill blocks allocated to each team.

We broke the design team down into groups, each representing a basic business unit based on a specific technology. The work groups recruited a few more representatives from their business units to assure well-rounded input and broaden ownership of the end product. We estimated as many as one hundred people involved in this portion of the design—most on a part-time basis; we still had a business to run.

The second requirement was negotiating a new labor contract to accurately represent our new vision, principles and work design. This moved smoothly because we had engaged the union from the beginning and directly involved a hundred people in the new design. When it came time to vote on the new contract, it was overwhelmingly approved on the first ballot.

The third requirement was a development approach for team leaders. To be honest, we didn't do so well here. We gave it a lick and a promise which served us okay at the beginning of the transition; but we found it necessary to return to the subject soon after launching the new system. On the second go we refined an excellent approach for developing leaders including effective assessment, development planning, follow-up and coaching/mentoring. In retrospect, I think this is the most important ingredient in establishing a new work/business system. We got away with doing less in the beginning because we had several managers with experience in the type of system we wanted to create. That is not always the case and it is quite often the reason attempts like ours fail.

The fourth requirement was a transition plan, a bridge from the old system to the new (specifically from the job classification system to our team-based skill block system). Our plan had to provide incentives for individuals to make the transition quickly while allowing for the basic differences from person to person.

Together, we developed an excellent approach that included an assessment of current skills, a development plan to acquire new skills (almost everyone needed additional skills), a certification system to assure these additional skills, and a fair timetable for attaining new skill blocks. Once an individual acquired the skills needed, he or she transitioned to the appropriate level in the new system.

The new level, at least for the first individuals to transition (generally the most capable workers), typically provided a higher rate of pay. Those who could not transition at a higher rate aimed at an equivalent rate with the opportunity to progress from there. We built in a provision that those who could not transition at an equivalent rate would be placed on the level most closely corresponding to their skill attainment. We allowed three years for employees to acquire a skill block certification; in hindsight I believe one to two years would have also been workable.

With each of these four requirements ready to go we were poised to launch our transition to the future we envisioned. To mark the start of this journey, and assure that each business unit was prepared, we established a rite of passage ceremony.

Each business unit had to have their design detail completed and approved by the original design team and me as the plant manager. We looked for the beginning of teamwork to support our basic business process, so each unit presented two examples of team interaction to improve the business in the form of a problem solved or an upgrade in their business process.

When a business unit met those requirements, we scheduled a meeting where a representative group met with the original design team for a final review of their efforts. Upon agreement by the design team that the business unit was ready, we gave the green light to begin the transition. By this point there was enough conversation and understanding within and between the business units that each of the final reviews resulted in passage on the first try.

So, the transition began, with a good bit of fanfare. The fanfare did not last long as the work of improving the performance of an aging pulp mill while at the same time overhauling the work system was plenty challenging for everyone involved. Some days it seemed like overhauling the engine in an over-the-road diesel big rig, while continuing a freight run at 70 miles an hour. It was exhilarating!

Chapter 10

Walking the Talk

❦

Involving a cross-section of people to develop a direction for our future, and designing a work system to accomplish it, had a very positive effect on the morale and commitment of the Foley organization. However, there were still too many folks in a wait-and-see mode for me to believe this would be enough to carry the organization through the transition.

These weren't bad people; most were very good. They liked the sound of our proposal—that wasn't the issue. The issue was, "will management see this through or abandon this for the next fad?" as had so often been the case in the past. The sustained consistency of leadership's engagement—or lack thereof—is what makes or breaks an organizational change effort. So, the success of this transition was up in the air.

The Move

A situation arose during the design effort that produced the first of many opportunities to walk the talk. Earl Belle was an hourly paid mechanic assigned to the design team. About halfway through the effort he and I talked about an aspect of the work system we were designing, and I mentioned some information I had in my office. The design team was meeting offsite, so I didn't have immediate access to a copy of the information for Earl.

So, I said to Earl, "Why don't you come to my office and I'll get you a copy?"

Earl replied, "Sure, where is your office?"

The plant facility was separated from the main office building by several hundred feet and a set of railroad tracks on which incoming materials were delivered and outgoing product shipped. So the picture was: big, ugly pulp mill where the workers worked; nice, clean office building where the managers did whatever it was they did, separated from the workers by the railroad tracks , which regularly had cars sitting between the mill and the office building.

Now, Earl had worked at Foley for several years. I thought it strange that he wouldn't know where the plant manager's office was; maybe he didn't realize I was the new plant manager, so I added, "You know Earl, the plant manager's office!"

Earl said, "But I don't know where that is: I've never been to the front office!"

Such a simple thing, and such an opportunity; I hadn't been thinking in terms of the industrial age. My mindset had always been based on the Cottage where everyone knew everyone and certainly knew where the plant manager's office was. But Earl was part of Frederick Taylor's scientific management system—a product of Theory X. He had spent his working years in his assigned box. He had no reason to ever go to the front office and had never been invited there (which was actually good news since individuals called to the front office were typically called in for a scolding or termination).

I gave Earl directions to my office. He came, we had a nice conversation; I gave him the information, and he left.

Simple enough, right? But, it wasn't so simple for me. That incident occupied my thoughts for several days. It underscored what was true for every employee in that plant—they were separate from management; separate from those who were supposed to lead them!

As I pondered this I began discussing my concern with the managers who reported to me—they represented the primary leadership of the business. An idea emerged. There were some offices inside the plant site that were under the domain of our junior engineers. What if we traded places with them? As we kicked the idea around, it began to take hold. But I was concerned about a couple of the managers who had been there for a long time; what were they thinking and how supportive would they be? After all, they had started off in those dingy workspaces and finally made it to the "front office" where they had windows for goodness sake! I remember the conversation I had with one of those experienced hands. His reaction was, "Great, let's do it; we're finally putting our words into action!" That sealed it for me, I trusted him to tell it straight. He was from the old school but willing to try a new way. His support gave me the confidence to press forward.

Since New Year's Day was coming up, we decided to use our move back to the plant as a symbol, not only of a new year, but a new era. We made the physical move on January 1st so we would be in place on the first business day of the New Year.

The result was remarkable. Most of the organization took a stroll through our space. We invited them into our offices to chat. Several commented that they had come over just to see if it was true—had we really made the move? Some asked if we still had our "normal" offices up front. We assured them we didn't—we were here to stay!

The word that perhaps best describes the general reaction in the organization is "impressed." People were impressed that we moved from more comfortable accommodations to be with them. The switch opened up a new level of respect and dialogue throughout the organization. That, coupled with our new work system design, formed a strong foundation from which to move forward.

This location switch wasn't part of a major strategy. We knew what we wanted to become and we had determined a set of guiding principles. Moving the management team to the plant started because an employee said, "I don't know where your office is; in fact, I have never been to the front office." That caused us to realize we had a built-in barrier to our principles, especially the ones that affirmed, "Things happen best when we work together" and "We care for each other and demonstrate mutual respect."

We had a built-in separation that clearly said "us" and "them." It made the statement, "We are the thinkers and decision makers; you are our hands." The move to the plant said, "You are important and you are where the action is. We will join you and help you be successful in what you are charged to do!" It didn't say how all of this would be done. But it did say, "We are in this together."

The Fight

More opportunities presented themselves—one just outside my new office. I might have missed it altogether had Dick Heydt not come in exclaiming, "John, are you aware of the fight that just occurred outside?" He pointed to an area between my office location and one of our maintenance shops.

He had my attention! "No, what fight?"

"Bobby Joe Green just decked Herbert Truesdale. Apparently Herbert and two of his cronies in the maintenance shop had been giving Bobby Joe a hard time about going to a Christmas party at Ben Morgan's house. As you know, Ben is an African American and they have been giving

Bobby Joe a fit about it. Apparently, Bobby Joe took all he was going to take and punched Herbert square in the face!"

"Can't say that I blame him, but that creates quite a problem."

"You've got that right, fighting means automatic loss of job according to the policy manual."

Our investigation discovered these two had been feuding for months. Herbert berated Bobby Joe with his vulgar racist comments, increasing in intensity and frequency as the clash continued. This only served to escalate the conflict.

There was a good deal more to this than just a fight between two angry workers. The whole organization watched to see how leadership would resolve the situation. On one hand, if we didn't discipline Bobby Joe for throwing the punch we would be condoning behavior that went against a long-standing policy that made sense. On the other hand, if we didn't do something to address Herbert's harassment, we would be turning a blind eye to his racist behavior.

We took our time, passing it through the grid of our principles as well as existing policies. As we deliberated, Bobby Joe and Herbert waited at home. We decided to give both men a two-week suspension without pay: Bobby Joe for throwing the punch; and Herbert for racist behavior and provoking the fight. At the same time we put out a strong message that we would not tolerate racist behavior of any type and that we also would not tolerate fighting.

They were required to attend counseling to address personal behavior changes. Then, we set up a discussion with each man, asking him to describe how he would comply with our principles in the future, especially the one that says, "We care for each other and demonstrate mutual support and respect."

Both assured me that we would never see this type of behavior again and that they were sorry for what they had done. I believed Bobby Joe was sincere, but I wasn't as sure about Herbert. He just didn't seem to value the principle of mutual support and respect as much.

About a year later an incident occurred that revealed a true change of heart for Herbert. Three employees, including Herbert, were busy repairing a piece of equipment—one of the workers was a woman. A contract employee from another company happened to be in our plant that day and called out something obscene to the woman. Herbert stopped the man and explained in no uncertain terms that his conduct went against our plant's principles. He insisted on an apology and a promise that it would never happen again. Not only did his reaction to this situation reflect our core values, I found it to be evidence of a true heart change when he referred to the principles as "our" principles. Apparently he decided to accept the policies as his own and, having accepted them, he spoke boldly to represent them on behalf of the other workers.

The Restaurant

Another incident occurred that struck at the heart of racial harmony of our organization. An African American from our corporate R&D group in Memphis was in our plant along with a few of his colleagues testing new product ideas. One evening they decided on dinner at a restaurant on the outskirts of town. They had heard the place served good food; what they weren't aware of was the place was more tavern than restaurant, and it didn't cater to African Americans.

Our people arrived at the restaurant and were denied access. There were heated words and a little pushing and shoving but to their credit our folks got out of there before something really bad happened.

This time it was Ken Stuparyk who brought me the news. We really didn't know what to do, but I recalled what John Feldman, my plant manager in Albany, Georgia did in similar circumstances. In Albany we experienced situations where African American managers were denied access to housing in apartment complexes with vacancies (easily verified by sending a white manager to ask for a rental application—without explaining the connection of course). With that knowledge in hand, John paid a visit to the owner or manager to talk about discrimination. It seldom took long to remedy the situation with apologies offered to our managers and properties made available after all.

Remembering that, I said to Ken (like I knew what I was doing), "Set up a meeting with the owner. Let's go have a chat with him."

A couple of days later Ken and I were on our way to visit this establishment. As we got into the car Ken said, "By the way, did you know that the owner is about six-five and weighs 260?"

I gasped, "Are you serious?"

"Serious as a heart attack!"

I didn't much care for the heart attack reference, but I got the drift. Then Ken said, "But look at this way, we each weigh about 170; so between us we outnumber him *and* outweigh him!"

"Thanks Ken, that really helps me relax. No fear, right?"

Fortunately, it was the middle of the afternoon so the tavern was nearly deserted when we arrived. That didn't calm my concerns; it meant very few witnesses—and none to take our side!

Ken had the owner's physical description right; he was big! We sat down with him in one of the booths, away from the bar area. I started off, "I guess you know why we are here?" I really didn't expect him to say "yes." I figured he'd act like he knew nothing, then, if anything, blame the incident on the poor help or something like that.

The owner responded, "Yeah, it's because of that group from the plant that came here the other night—the ones we wouldn't let in, right?"

His response surprised me, but I figured he had something up his sleeve, like they were at capacity. So, I followed up with another question, "Yes, it is about that group and the fact that they were turned away. My understanding is that they were turned away because one of the individuals was black. Is that true?"

I fully expected him to deny the claim, but to our surprise he admitted this was the case. In fact he said it was his wife who turned them away and then he added that she was right to do it. He explained, "I see it as a matter of life or death. If we allowed the black guy in, there probably would have been a fight, maybe a shooting, and someone, probably him, would have been killed. So the way I see it, my wife saved his life!"

Ken asked, "Do you realize that what you are doing is against the law?"

He responded, "You're new around here, aren't you? This is the way it is. We've been getting along just fine, each knowing their place, black and white. Those laws just mess up things. Like I said, if we followed it like you want, we'd wind up with a killin'. Now which is worse?"

We were stunned by his logic and his arrogance. Clearly we weren't going to get anywhere with this guy, but I at least wanted to voice my opinion. Exasperated, I said, "I don't know what kind of place you are running, but I don't accept your rationale for treating people the way you do. The individuals I work with believe in the principle of treating all people with respect and dignity. I see no reason why you shouldn't do the same."

I thought he might let me have the last word, but of course he couldn't leave well enough alone. He said, "That's the way it is here, gentlemen. I realize you can turn me in and get me shut down, but I've told you like it is."

As we walked away I thought, "That isn't the way it worked in Albany. So much for an apology and an invitation back!" I said to Ken, "Well, he's got one thing right."

"What's that?"

"We're going to turn him in and get him shut down!"

And we certainly tried. We enlisted the support of various government agencies and made a good run at it, but in the end the best we accomplished was a letter of apology from the establishment to each of the individuals they turned away that night. Also, the owner posted a non-discrimination statement on the wall near the front door. All was not lost.

It wasn't nearly what I wanted to accomplish but it had a profound effect on our organization. News of the encounter spread. Our actions, coupled with the fight incident and everything else we did at the plant, left no question in anyone's mind where we as leaders stood on the subject of discrimination and on the principle of treating everyone with respect and dignity. We might not be able to change the outside world as much as we wanted, but we would stand up for what we believed, and we would stand up for the people following us.

Turning Loose

All of this caused the organization to become more and more committed to the new direction, fulfilling more of our principles. We promoted concepts like: "Every employee is an owner" and, "Every member of our diverse workforce is encouraged and allowed to contribute to our business. Each shares in the personal satisfaction and rewards that come from this."

At some point coaches simply have to let go and let the team play the game. We had designed a work system that embodied the shared principles of our organization. Now was the time to turn it loose. This wasn't so hard with some areas, like the basic operational tasks, but some areas were harder to let go of, like making decisions and interacting with customers.

Early in the transition, this was really brought home to me. Tennessee Eastman of the Eastman Chemical Company was a potential new customer. As part of the sales pitch we shared our experiences on the subject of empowered, high-involvement organizations. We decided to host a visit by the key people at Eastman Chemical, starting with Ernie Davenport, the CEO. The presidents of the various divisions of Eastman would join Ernie at Foley, so the visit became known as the presidents' visit. Obviously, it was a big deal to us.

Tennessee Eastman had huge potential in an area of business new to us, so there was a lot on the line. We hoped they would be so impressed by our new work system that they would accept us as a major supplier of cellulose fiber.

The plan included a tour of the facility and presentations on our technology capabilities. We arranged for a cross section of the people involved in developing the organizational design to do that part of the presentation. To set this up we described our intent to the original design team.

One of the members of that team was a fellow by the name of Richard Allison. Richard was a mechanic and one of the few individuals who actually volunteered for the design team. The reason he volunteered is that he was highly frustrated with the way things were going and wanted to make a difference. Richard was very bright and his communication style was confrontational. This led to strong interactions (read that as arguments) on a regular basis. I was often unsure if Richard was with us or against us, and it's likely he didn't know either as he tried to sort out his view on various topics.

We always allowed Richard to have his say and, once we got past the bluster, he proved to be quite insightful. As we grew to understand each other, everyone on the team valued

Richard more and more. Likewise, Richard learned to be a little smoother as he experienced our acceptance of him and received our appreciation for his thoughts and ideas.

When we described what we wanted to do for the presidents' visit, Richard volunteered to make a presentation on our new work system. I felt a twinge in my gut, and my brain said, "Oh no, not Richard! There's no telling what tangent he's apt to take off on!" I had come to like Richard, and I valued him. But I was not yet ready to give him the keys to the car and let him drive on this project!

But I really had no choice. We were inviting our people to help us close the deal with a major new prospect, and here I was thinking about telling one of them—who had made one of the largest contributions to the design effort—"No thanks!" I couldn't do it. I would have to let go and trust Richard to do it well. I knew he could; I just wasn't sure if he would.

Our plan included Richard as one of six presenters. Each would describe a different aspect of the new work system, then the six would act as a panel for a question and answer period.

The big day came, and it was going great right up to the panel discussion. I started getting nervous. The first individual spoke and responded to a couple of questions, then the second. Richard was slated last to speak. I looked at him and he grinned back at me. He gave a little thumbs-up sign; he knew I was nervous.

When the time came, Richard was fantastic. I have never heard anyone do any better in a presentation to VIPs nor have I ever heard a better sales pitch. He didn't overdo it, it was just right. During the question and answer period it was clear who the key guy was—Richard. He didn't dominate the discussion (which he had been known to do); he was very balanced and on target with all of his comments.

As I sat there, marveling, I thought, "John, you dummy! You invited these people to participate in finding new business. Why doubt them? Why think they would be any less invested in this process than you? Of course Richard excelled—we set him up for success, *not* failure."

I think about that experience often. Richard helped me become much better at letting go and letting others have a shot at demonstrating their own capability and willingness to be responsible.

Richard was eventually recruited away from us to be a manager in a new paper mill startup. He later moved to human resources and wrote a book on his experiences, which I proudly display in my office bookcase.

The Raisins

There is one more story worth telling from a little later in the transition effort. Historically, there had been an Annual Management Dinner, a coat and tie affair with cocktails, dinner, and a speech from a high ranking Procter and Gamble executive. As the name indicates, it was a manager-only function.

Company-wide Procter and Gamble changed that to The Business Dinner and opened it up to all employees. The change occurred at the same time we were beginning our transition, so it provided a built-in opportunity for us to walk the talk.

We determined we didn't want to follow the tried and true formula for such dinners: cocktails, dinner, and speech. We wanted to do something fresh and appropriate for our emerging culture where everyone works together to accomplish our objectives.

We labored over this quite a bit before we hit on an approach. It was Dave Fraser, our accounting manager, who came up with the coup de grace. Dave and his family are very creative and musically talented—forget the dull accountant stereotype. Rather than list our preparation efforts, I'll describe the end result.

The affair was held in the National Guard Armory—the community had no other venue large enough to accommodate a group our size. We started with a social time outside the hall before welcoming everyone in at once. The place had been transformed into a dinner theater. I kicked off the festivities with a few comments and introduced our guest speaker, a Procter and Gamble vice president who congratulated the organization on what they had achieved in the transition of the business.

Then dinner was served: Delmonico steaks and all the fixings. A small ensemble provided dinner music. As people finished dessert, Elvena Johnson, an administrative technician in the public relations department, approached the podium. "Ladies and gentlemen," she announced. "To conclude our business event tonight we have one more presentation to make. We have researched our entire organization and learned that we have five employees who have professional caliber entertainment skills. We have coaxed them to perform for you tonight. Would you please give the 'Foley Raisins' a warm welcome and your undivided attention."

At that point music, recorded by one of our talented young managers, began: "I heard it through the grapevine, Foley folks are really fine..." The curtains parted and out danced five members of our leadership team. It wasn't easy to tell who was who, because each of us appeared as giant raisins. At first there was a silence in the audience, then folks realized who the "crazies" onstage were and a howl of laughter, hooting and hollering broke out. The routine got rave reviews!

A few weeks later we were describing all this to a visitor who said, "I can see where that was a lot of fun, but how in the world would that help you improve business results?"

110

I responded, "Well, first of all, to get the business results we need, we have to get everyone in the game and playing to their full ability. One of the things we have to overcome is the gap that exists between management and the organization. We made prior progress through the other things we were doing, but this one event really catapulted our intent. It was the first time all employees were invited to what had previously been a management-only function. Because of our willingness to act like fools together, we appeared more down to earth in the eyes of our employees.

"As a matter of fact, we noticed a marked improvement in the comfort level of our organization toward us. We can't translate that precisely into a bottom line effect, but we do know our bottom line is improving, and we know the people in our organization are more committed than ever to continuing that improvement. Anything we can do to eliminate barriers to working together has got to be directionally right!"

We saw progress in numerical outcomes while we were still in transition. We reduced total cost by 22 percent—a huge improvement. We made a three-fold improvement in quality by reducing variability and increasing control over key attributes of our product to the target established by our customers—resulting in more business.

Bringing "Heart" Back to Leadership

These stories highlight two key messages about successful leadership. First, the people around you will make or break you; everyone knows that. So the second message is really the most important. The people around you want to be successful too, and they are willing to follow your lead if you deal with life's opportunities and curve balls in a principled, consistent way. If people can trust you to be who you say you are and do what you say you will do, and if you'll give them a chance to do what they are capable of doing, they will make you successful in return.

The problem often is too many voices—too many demands and challenges, including life's curve balls. Many leaders go through life reacting to all these voices, instead of acting on the organization's shared principles, steadily moving forward, proactively dealing with the challenges they see ahead and staying consistent on the curve balls they didn't see coming.

This is why it is so important that we return to the Cottage. Without the foundation of those principles, all of our efforts to manage and lead are mechanistic—all mental and physical, head and hands, but no heart. Returning to the Cottage means bringing the heart back into everything we do!

Chapter 11

Curve Ball

❧ ❧

About the time we got the business really humming, Procter and Gamble threw us a curve that, frankly, felt like being hit by an emotional freight train.

Finally, just as we made the kind of return on investment other P&G divisions made (and that's tough in a company that produces soap, toothpaste and mouthwash), they decided to sell the pulp business. The Foley organization was shocked—then angry—then numb. Our people had never known another company.

At this point I took the morning walk I described at the beginning of this story. I came awfully close to throwing in the towel that day but the values and principles I learned in my family's Cottage business made it impossible to quit. No other choice but to keep on keeping on.

Here is where we would learn the true capability of our organization—what we were really made of! Now we could determine the practical outcomes of our work system to see how it worked in real-time situations. Initially, not so well, to everyone's shock and dismay. We were proud of our corporate parent and we felt like we were being thrown out of the family. Abandoned. Rejected.

To give credit where due, our people stoically kept the place running, and after processing the news for a few days, they began to say, "We're being sold, not shut down. This means we'll have a new owner, but it will still be up to us to make it a successful business. Let's put our best foot forward and attract the best buyer we can and convince whoever it is that we know what we are doing."

And that's what they did. In fact the technicians got their act together faster than most of the managers, many of whom had staked their careers on being with Procter and Gamble until retirement. It took these managers a couple of weeks longer to move from dazed to productive, and during that time the technicians essentially carried the organization.

Business results continued to improve through the divestiture (about a year) and beyond. The new owners had to pay more for the business than they would have a few years earlier, but they received a very profitable business with the capability to continue the improvement trend and supply talent to other parts of a new company.

Throughout this process I held the general manager role over the whole business unit—a role that did not survive the sale. I had the option to continue with Procter and Gamble, but after nearly 30 years in industry, I decided it was time to test my entrepreneurial skills. But before I tell that part of the story I would like to conclude with an account a group of visitors wrote a year later. It provides a pretty good picture of the final result of our work there.

The Result

It's Monday afternoon as we approach the manufacturing site for the Buckeye Florida Corporation [the new name for the business]. As we drive up we notice that the lawns and shrubbery are neat and manicured, and the building exterior is well maintained. We park and walk to the main entrance where we are greeted by Ed Jones, who is prepared for our arrival and has come from his work area to greet us. He's a friendly fellow and makes us feel welcome as he explains the safety considerations we need to understand before touring the facility.

As the tour begins we can't help but be impressed with the cleanliness and orderliness of the facility. We've been told that it's about 50 years old, yet it looks great—almost like new. As we move along we notice people working diligently at a variety of tasks. It's not possible to tell managers from workers or any particular craft group from another. What is noticeable, however, is the fact that the people we see represent a lot of diversity. There are men and women and different races working harmoniously together. Everyone is friendly and helpful.

In the manufacturing areas we notice a continuation of the neatness and orderliness, and it appears that the process itself is very well organized—it's running smoothly with no evidence of scrap or waste material anywhere. In various places there are information boards with neatly arranged graphs showing various kinds of information for the process, feedback from customers and other business information. The trends for the information look very positive. Ed, our host, confirms this with additional information that indicates world-class performance for a number of key factors like process reliability, maintenance reliability, percentage of good product, etc. Ed's knowledge level is quite impressive, made even more so when we learn that he is an hourly paid employee or "technician" as they are called.

As we walk further we come upon a group of individuals standing around a flip chart, engaged in a discussion. We take care not to interrupt; but listen in for a moment —apparently the group is trying to determine how to tackle a process issue they are faced with. There are three individuals and one of them seems to be in charge. They aren't arguing but the discussion is spirited as each conveys their point of view.

Now the one who seems to be the leader is summarizing, and the other two are agreeing. Looks like they've got it resolved and are breaking up to go back to their process. We ask Ed if we can speak to the leader for a moment, and he says, "Sure, go right ahead."

So I call out to the individual who seems to be running things, "Excuse me ma'am, could you tell us what was going on in your meeting?"

"Sure, I'd be glad to! By the way, my name is Sue Martin, and I work here in the finishing department. Our statistical process information is indicating a slight drift in one of our key variables, so we were putting our heads together for a minute to decide what to do about it. We don't have enough data points yet to indicate a real trend, so we'll monitor it for a little longer, but we're set up to deal with it if we have to."

"Sounds like you have everything under control. By the way, I notice that you are kind of running things—are you the manager?"

"No," she answers. "I'm a technician. One of the skill blocks I'm qualified in is the final packaging operation. That's where we are noticing the potential problem, so it's up to me to start the problem-solving sequence. We try to catch things before they become a problem; that's why we had this quick little meeting. Joe and Bill each operate the equipment that produces the product that comes to my area for packaging, and it's possible that something in their area is affecting the package quality, so I wanted to be sure they were alerted to the possibility and are looking out for it."

She continues, "You see, I'm also qualified in the skill block for the equipment they are operating and last week, when I was working over there, I noticed the same thing. We were able to easily correct it, and I wanted to be sure they were aware of it."

There is much more we would like to ask, but we end the conversation to let Sue get back to her responsibilities.

As our tour continues, Ed invites us to stop and talk with anyone we'd like to—so we do, several times. The friendliness and willingness of the people to answer our questions is really impressive. As with Sue, we learn that all the employees are multi-skilled and they stay current in all of them by doing them on a regular basis. This gives them a very thorough understanding of their part of the process, which is of great benefit in solving problems and generating new ideas to improve operations.

We also note that each employee is very knowledgeable about the overall business—especially the customers. In fact, several mention they have visited their customer's process and observed first-hand how well their product is performing.

We realize after talking to several people that we had not talked to a mechanic or electrician so we make a point to ask about that. We are told that several of the technicians qualified in a maintenance skill block, which allows them to do basic maintenance in their process. Because of this there is no need to call on maintenance specialists for most of the things that occur on shift. If they do run into something they can't handle there are maintenance technicians who have more advanced skill blocks that can be called on for support, but this happens very infrequently. The advanced maintenance technicians spend most of their time either working in the core process to keep their skills up or working on technical projects to improve the process.

The other thing we realize is that we had not talked to any managers—at least as far as we could tell. We ask Ed, "Where are the managers?"

Ed chuckles and says, "That's a question everyone who tours finally asks. As we've toured there have been a few managers around but they don't look any different than the technicians in the organization. They are very important to our overall success. Come on, I'll introduce you to some, and you can quiz them all you want."

Ed introduces us to Sam Baker, who is one of the process team managers, and Ellen Fitzgerald, who is the technical support manager in the area. Ed tells Sam and Ellen that we finally realized we hadn't met a manager yet and wondered if they even exist!

Sam responds with laughter. "We intentionally let the technicians handle the day-to-day operation, including visitors. Our role as managers is to coach, much like you see in sports. We are responsible to develop the team and each individual on the team, but we don't play the game for them, we let them do it. Of course, we are available to help and we are always thinking of ways to improve the team."

One of our group comments, "That makes sense, but in sports, like football, there is someone on the field called the quarterback who calls the signals."

Ellen jumps in and says, "You've just completed the analogy; that's exactly what happens here. One person on the team functions as the quarterback, or team leader as we call them. They rotate the responsibility among several who have developed this team leader skill. The people on the team respond to the team leader during the shift (game time), but look to the team manager (the coach) for overall direction and development."

Another of our group asks, "When a person is functioning as team leader is that the total job?"

Sam responds, "No, just like the quarterback on the football team, our team leader plays a regular position. Also we have other leadership responsibilities that others fulfill for things like safety and training. It's a system of shared leadership."

"What happens if a conflict between two people emerges, who takes care of that?"

"The teams have been trained to deal with conflict and several on each team have pretty good skills in that area. I'd say that the teams themselves solve 95% of all interpersonal conflicts. However, if they can't handle it they will call one of us and we get involved with them, not so much to resolve it ourselves but rather to help them work through it," Ellen replies.

We talk a bit more with Sam and Ellen before saying goodbye. It's time to leave—even though it seems like we just arrived. As Ed walks to the front entrance with us I ask him what he will do after we left.

"Well, I've got to brush up on some training material because tomorrow I will be spending the morning training a group of new employees on the principles of our work system. Then it's back to my team and my regular duties. I really enjoy being involved in training new people, because when I retire, I'll be counting on the stock I've accumulated while working here. So, it's real important that these new folks get a good start and keep this place performing well in the future."

As we drive away, one of the individuals in our group comments, "You know, I didn't see a single person loafing. Everyone we saw was truly in the game playing; that was impressive."

Another chimes in, "I agree, somehow they've developed a way of working together that is focused on the right things yet flexible enough to effectively deal with changes and issues as they emerge. It works very well and appears to have the stability to do well on into the future."

Summary of Change

Each time I've taken folks to observe the Foley operation, I've proudly recounted the vision we established years earlier. They witnessed something remarkably similar to the vision that seemed such a stretch when we first started out.

Foley is still a large manufacturing operation, a vestige of the Industrial Age, but there is something different about it—something Cottage-like. We changed the culture of the plant in ways that endure. The spirit of the place, the collegial atmosphere, the can do attitude, small teams of committed workers with leaders who coach and develop people—that's what brought the difference to the bottom line. The values of the Cottage brought back the heart—the realization that it still takes people to get anything done. To quote my father, "if it's worth doing it's worth doing right!"

Chapter 12

Transition

❧ ☙

January 2, 1995

I woke up this morning earlier than usual, after a restless night. After 50 years of being productive, each morning promising great opportunities and adventure, I woke up unemployed and unsure of my next step—dazed, almost surreal. Perhaps symptoms of this new, unfamiliar life of mine—feeling anxious, even a little fear. Or maybe my symptoms were of something much more benign, like a cold or allergies acting up.

This new beginning wasn't forced upon me. I hadn't been fired or lost my job due to a business closing, although the business I managed had been sold. My job was eliminated but I wasn't asked to leave—that was my own doing. In fact, a high-placed officer of the company presented an opportunity for me to join an emerging business in Russia. He said I would probably do better in a situation like that than a role at corporate headquarters because of my entrepreneurial spirit. I decided to decline. It was time to move on. Neither my father nor grandfather worked for anyone. They had their own businesses, a carryover from the "Cottage Age." I had grown up in the Cottage life, and always thought I had it in my blood to do something on my own.

But I had moved from the cottage to the corporation at an early age and found that I was pretty good at corporate dealings. I moved up steadily to some very challenging responsibilities and performed well, including my last position. So when the business sold I took the opportunity to move on— to create my own trail. Without my day planned for me, I didn't feel particularly enthusiastic about my new position in life. The adventure part hadn't exactly kicked in yet. Would it ever? What had I done?

I left a great company, a promising career, and pretty good money to create my own trail. I probably should have had my head examined. My decision didn't make sense when measured up to common definitions for success. I made a mental calculation as to where I would have been eventually if I had stayed with the company—It didn't help me any!

As that first unemployed workday proceeded, I gathered my thoughts a little, mostly to reassure myself that I had always done well and certainly some of what I learned and experienced in the first half of my adult life would transfer nicely into the second half. However, being an action person, I wanted clarity on how this new life would shape up. I needed to see it in my mind's eye to know I made the right choice. I had the feeling it wouldn't become clear overnight.

I recalled an incident that occurred several years earlier. I had just completed my first assignment with Procter and Gamble as a team manager (shift supervisor) for fourteen technicians manufacturing Pampers disposable diapers (Chapter 5). I thought I had done well and expected to be promoted to the next level—what the company called a department manager, a role responsible for four team leaders and their teams as well as the whole 24-hour operation. It didn't happen. Instead of being promoted to that role, I was given a project manager role I didn't really want. I was miffed to say the least.

A couple of months later my previous boss, Wayne Richards, asked if he could talk to me privately. I respected him a lot and thought maybe he would bale me out of the situation. When I got to his office he looked at me like he was upset and asked, "What are you doing, John?" No "hello, how are you" —just a blunt question that matched the look on his face.

Being an occasional smart mouth I retorted, "I'm just doing this lousy job!"

His response to that was, "The only thing I see that is lousy about that job is the way you are doing it." It was one of those comments that don't register immediately.

As I formulated another smart-mouth retort, it finally registered and stopped me in my tracks. Now, thanks to an attitude adjustment, I was in the right frame of mind to receive what he had to say. "What do you mean?" I asked.

He told me it was clear I didn't like the job because it showed. It showed in my attitude and it showed in the results—or lack of results. It hit me. He spoke the truth. It was obvious I didn't like what I was doing but it hadn't dawned on me that I performed poorly because of my negative attitude. He warned me—if I didn't get my act together I would not be employed much longer.

Now that did two things to me. It made me mad and at the same time it scared me. As I left his office I determined to do two things. I would quit the company; but I would not quit as a loser. I would work to be successful and gain back my reputation, and then I would quit.

The end result is no surprise. I did work hard and finally did well in the assignment. Eventually I became that department manager I wanted to be—but most of all I learned a defining lesson that marked me for life. I'm guessing we've all fought moments when we struggle with doing well or feel like quitting and moving on. Anytime I fought a moment of weakness like that, I'd remember that incident and reset myself to work with all my energy to be successful. I determined I would try some more, and if by next year things weren't better, then I'd quit. That delay tactic always worked and I stayed with the company for many years.

So here I was—I had quit I guess, but not because I struggled with a moment of weakness. On the contrary, I transitioned when I was at the top of my game. I had the highest regard for my company, Procter and Gamble. The question now was, transition to what? The only way to find out was to get moving and do the best I could do in terms of investigating opportunities. I knew I wanted to return to the Cottage somehow. I wanted to find a way to do something entrepreneurial, to feel the satisfaction of creating something new and different.

Later that week, a good friend asked me to go with him to help sell a consulting concept to a prospective client. He was an organizational change consultant himself and had built a pretty good business doing that with a variety of companies. I asked him what he wanted me to do and he said, "Just talk about what you've been doing for the past several years. Most companies don't do what you know how to do."

I went with him and spent a couple of hours in this meeting. My friend conducted most of the pitching, but I contributed some thoughts based on my experience. I don't think he got the contract but I saw something that day and it began a thought process for me that has influenced me greatly in my second half.

I didn't move in that direction right away. I considered other options first, like buying an existing business. I worked with a business broker and actually made an offer on one. I followed all the standard advice to purchasing a business, such as how to determine the best starting offer based on the asking price, and requesting the current owner hold a note for part of the money. These concepts worked to begin negotiations. I had bargained contracts with unions so I was somewhat familiar with the process. This proposal felt like tennis moves—I put the ball in his court and he sent it back with some movement toward me but not all the way. I expected several volleys before it came together. Well, his response was no movement. He wanted full price and no further involvement of any kind. The business was very successful making a niche product for well-known customers so he probably believed he could get his price. Perhaps he could—but it stopped me cold. I became very uncomfortable going further.

At about this point I met with my accountability group of businessmen. During the meeting I described all of this, how I felt on my first day of unemployment, the consulting visit, my attempt to buy a business—all of it. Their response surprised me but got my attention. "John, are you crazy, why are you trying to buy a business? We are all trying to sell ours and we envy you. Do something that takes advantage of what you know. Use that to teach others. You'll have very little expenses and virtually no overhead, both of which is a constant struggle for us to cover in our businesses."

As I headed into the next year I began to focus on that advice and the more I considered it the more I understood a couple of important things. I began to realize more fully what I was all about, what God had put into me when He created me, and how I could best use that skill-set. I found myself becoming purposeful again—a purpose of coming alongside leaders and helping them do what they felt in their hearts to do. It was no longer to lead something, which was my professional purpose in the first half. Now it was to help others lead something, and in a way, to multiply the assets and experience God had given me.

A Company of One

I joined the ranks of an interesting category of businesses—the US census refers to it as "single person owned businesses." There are over 20 million of these according to the 2006 census. In many ways this is the "Cottage Industry" of our millennium. This is how it happened.

I was at the "halftime" of my professional life, and like others who come to this point, I was trying to figure out what I wanted to do with the second half. I was eager to try something new, something that took advantage of things already learned but in a new context... something significant!

As I thought and prayed through all of that I put together three ideas. The first was something those men in my accountability group encouraged me to do. I would use my experience and knowledge from the first half to help other business leaders. Since I had been involved in manufacturing start-ups I could provide an expertise known as "change management" which includes both organizational techniques along with technical process techniques—all aimed at developing highly reliable and productive manufacturing processes.

Secondly, I would tap the skills and capabilities of others moving into the second half—others who thought similarly to me and offered different skills and capabilities from mine. Thirdly, I decided to form a company that allowed me to function as a sole proprietor yet contract others as I needed them for various projects. In effect this would be a catalyst for the formation of other "sole proprietor" companies—other "companies of one."

There was only one small detail left—for whom would I offer my services? As with all business ventures this became *the* issue, of course. I named my business, *The Business Resource Network*, and it was clear to me that I would network with others to find other service-providers. Next, I needed to find clients. I started making calls. One of the calls I made was to a former colleague from P&G who was now with International Paper. I knew he had something to do with the efforts to develop their organizational capability. This turned out to be a most fortuitous call because it linked me to some key individuals who had need of what I could offer and led to a five year run of work with this company in several of their manufacturing locations. It also provided the opportunity to link in several other consultants at various times for these projects, when the needs fell outside my particular specialties.

This provided a foundation of business for my new enterprise. From there I also contracted work with several other smaller companies that tended to be private and entrepreneur led. The combination provided a wonderful opportunity to contrast the difference between corporate America and SMEs (small, medium enterprises) that were led by entrepreneurs.

Transition Two—2001

I had just transitioned to my "company of one" when another transition occurred. Interestingly it occurred when the whole country, indeed the world, experienced an event that transformed how all of us live—what we refer to as 9-11, and many would refer to as the beginning of the "war on terror." No, I was not at the World Trade Center that day but my life was changing at that same point.

To tell this part of my story I must digress. Several years earlier, when we lived in Germany, we met Paul and Phyllis Stanley. Paul and Phyllis introduced us to a whole new world. They showed us a world of people who struggle to eke out an existence in areas where earning income was far more difficult than for most in the United States. And once we witnessed that world with our own eyes, we knew we had to help. Kathie and I were impacted by the selflessness of this couple and others with whom they worked. Eventually, it led to a trip to the former Soviet Union countries of Slovakia,

Hungary and Romania. I took the trip just to see what it was like—I had no idea what I would find.

A surprising discovery—the people in these countries were not only very interested in me, but what I did professionally. At the end of the Soviet control the culture abruptly changed from communism to free enterprise—with virtually no preparation. People were forced to figure out how to provide for themselves. All forms of enterprise were tried to do that—not all positive or successful, of course. They had many questions, some fairly simple and some very complex, but they wanted to hear what a businessperson from America had to say.

This led to several trips to the region. I helped start up a consulting company. Later I traveled several times with leaders from the region to provide consulting advice to small startup enterprises. Sometimes other American businessmen accompanied me, and we developed an approach to assess each small business we encountered. Then we provided feedback from this assessment along with ideas for how the enterprise could be further developed. We also taught these skills to loan officers involved in micro enterprise and SME (small medium enterprise) development. Our purpose was to teach them skills that would equip them to be more involved in these emerging new businesses.

This consultation work has continued in various ways and has taken me to many countries around the world. I estimate that I've been involved with over 100 small companies internationally, which provides a great deal of insight to a growing trend in America and indeed around the world. I see a trend for our next generations to be entrepreneurial (more on that later).

As this part of my consulting business developed, the dot-com bubble burst and we fell into a recessional period. This affected the Pulp and Paper industry in terms of falling prices and a squeeze on profits. With threats to profits, the industry is quick to reduce costs. That includes jettisoning consulting help, which is not considered essential (in this industry) when times are tight money-wise. This represented about 80% of my business at the time.

At about the same time the organization that Paul and Phyllis Stanley were a part of (a nonprofit called The Navigators) decided to rethink and reset their organizational purpose. I was asked to facilitate the effort. I spent the next 2 years helping them accomplish that transition. I facilitated several meetings with emerging leaders in a variety of locations around the world. This would have never happened if I was still involved with International Paper—I wouldn't have had the time or the networks in place. My "second half" was shaping up and my life purpose was being redefined with these new opportunities.

The experience transformed me. At first, I felt completely out of my element, but came to see that the skills I learned in the corporate manufacturing environment were useful in this totally different professional environment. This realization had the same "light bulb effect" as learning that people in the former Soviet Union were interested in what I had to say. I began to realize that although each person we meet is different there are some common principles and concepts that apply organizationally no matter our location, position or business. It brought a note of reality to the scripture, "We are made in God's image." There are some common denominators. From a perspective of wanting to help people be successful in their endeavors, these common denominators provide great direction to design (or redesign) organizations.

During this same period I met an older man who had created a business around coaching young leaders. At any point in time, he worked with about 12 leaders. He met with each on a monthly basis and helped them process their thoughts and dreams, and then devise and implement an action plan. As I shared what I did, he pointed out that I essentially coached people in the same way. I didn't impose my thoughts as to what they should do, rather I believed they already knew —at least they possessed a seed idea. What others needed from me is help and encouragement to figure out <u>how</u> to proceed with their ideas.

I was ready to re-launch my business with this newfound life application of my experience and knowledge. I needed to crank up the networking and as I focused on re-starting, the network came to me. Within two weeks two individuals called me, each one linking me to a business where my skills could be utilized. One was a pulp and paper industry company where I have been able to apply my knowledge and experience regarding organizational change and the other, a start up entrepreneur-led company where I have been able to utilize and further develop my coaching capabilities.

As this took place I also increased my work with The Navigators in the area of enterprise development around the world, building on the work started in the former Soviet Union countries a few years earlier.

What I've Learned

    A. There is an emerging generation of entrepreneurs that have much passion to do something on their own. As generations before them, it is common for entrepreneurs to stumble as they get started, but this resurgence of Cottage Industry will reset the bar for generations to come. I have also learned that the information age has a great deal to offer this movement. In fact, they are inseparable.

    B. I have also learned much about leading, and especially about being an entrepreneur. I believe there are foundational aspects that must be understood and present in order to be successful and I'm convinced that they are quite often missing from business strategy.

The Emerging Entrepreneurial Generation
(The following stories chronicle my learning.)

Jim just completed college. After a few twists and turns he settled on a major in Business Management with a concentration in Entrepreneurism. He is a very talented young man in a number of ways and could have gone a number of different directions, but he continued to find himself thinking and dreaming about doing something on his own as an entrepreneur. He and his buddies talked of little else. Their conversations always flowed to an idea one of them had regarding a business venture.

One such idea was to provide a service for the football fans of the university he attended. He noticed an opportunity regarding the growing phenomenon known as tailgating—the pregame party in the parking lot or on the lawns of the campus. The business would provide a service that organized all aspects of the party for a group of fans in a way that allowed them to just show up—instant tailgate party! They didn't have to get there early to reserve a spot, they didn't have to bring food and they didn't have to bring tables, chairs or their big screen TV (yes, some never do make it to the game). Jim arranged it all and he did it for many different fan groups. He couldn't do this by himself so he organized a group of underclassmen as staff. He identified vendors who could supply him what he needed when he needed it. Oh, and one more thing—he was paid very well for each tailgate party he set up.

Now Jim faces a dilemma, one of many he'll likely face during his entrepreneurial career. He is no longer a student, he has graduated, but he has this business started. Should he stay with it and build it up or should he move on to the next thing? Between the scholastic studies regarding entrepreneurism and experience already under his belt—the future certainly holds many more exciting things for Jim to conquer.

How often does this story—and others like it—occur? Some studies suggest that half of all college students say they don't want to work for anyone; they want to chart their own course as an entrepreneur. Some will be well prepared, like Jim, but many will not be. What is it that drives this generation to want to be entrepreneurial?

Most of us suspect it is their observation of the generations that have gone before them and the way they have been treated (and mistreated) by corporations. Many have likely seen a family member lose their job unexpectedly, and have observed close-up the wounds caused by employment drama.

In addition, we hear more and more stories of successful entrepreneurs starting up information age companies—as well as a whole variety of support businesses necessary to keep it all going. Everyone understands that the failure rate is high for startup companies but most young adults don't let that sway them from trying.

There are some who figure out a way to do it by combining their entrepreneurial ambition and a job with an existing company. Branden was such a person. He had always wanted to do something entrepreneurial but he began his professional career with a company that had a successful start-up several years earlier. That scratched the entrepreneurial itch somewhat but not enough. Branden had a passion to do something more—and to do it as an entrepreneur. He decided to start a restaurant but knew from the beginning he would not have the time to do both that and continue the job he held, which he really liked and didn't want to give up just yet. In order to pursue this dream he collaborated with other individuals he knew he could trust. They put together a business plan, raised some money (from his friends and family network) and got started.

The restaurant is doing very well today and Branden is continuing to enjoy success in his role with his employer. I asked him why he picked a restaurant to start up, wondering if he had some sort of background in the food-service industry. He said he did not have experience. What he had was a passion to do something different and he picked starting a restaurant knowing he would have to collaborate with others regardless of his business choice. He also determined not to be the "general manager" of this business because of his other responsibilities — he believed he could influence what needed to be done from a major shareholder point of view. So far it has worked out well for Branden.

Others don't set out to start a company — they are simply thrust into being entrepreneurial. When a company downsizes and "early-retires" some individuals, starting their own businesses may be their only alternative. When the situation changed in countries like Slovakia and other central European countries as a result of the end of Russian occupation and communism, people scrambled to find a way to survive and provide for their families. Many moved in the direction of being entrepreneurial — they started small businesses.

Milan Cicel had been educated in Bratislava, Slovakia as a control engineer and had a PhD. During the Soviet control he worked for a state-owned company (as they all were). The company was involved in the wood products industry and Milan developed several technological innovations that earned him awards. When communism fell and the Soviets moved out these companies were privatized and, for the most part, wound up in the hands of former communist leaders who now proclaimed themselves to be in favor of free enterprise. The entire situation was precarious and people like Milan, who never had accepted the communist ideologies, were left out in the cold. They had to find a different way.

Milan and 3 others decided to combine their skills and capabilities by forming a consulting company. They saw a need to help the emerging businesses — both those being privatized and those being newly created—learn how to cope in this new world they found themselves in. To do that they requested and received help from several "western" business individuals who had experience doing what they needed to do. I was one of the ones privileged to be involved with them in those beginning years of free enterprise.

The consulting company became successful and is to this day. But the most interesting thing is the impact created beyond just what his business accomplished. Essentially, these same individuals who initiated the consulting company created an approach to facilitate the development of more entrepreneurial companies. Now, almost 20 years later, there are over a thousand micro enterprises and SMEs (small/medium enterprises) throughout the region of Central Europe as a result of their effort, and the number continues to grow.

I find the character of Milan Cicel to be very interesting. He was never in it to make money or be successful. He was in it to help the people around him survive in a new world where jobs weren't merely handed out. That was his passion. He knew he could never do it by himself—he needed to join with others. Actually, it was others that put most of the approaches, plans and implementation strategies together, but it was Milan's heart that got it started and in many ways sustained it.

More Entrepreneurial Stories

Timothy Mahinda is a Kenyan who had an idea to develop an insurance agency in the city of Nairobi that would be known as "the honest insurance agency." He had a slight problem however. To look like the professional he wanted to be he needed a suit and shoes but didn't have the money to buy them. So he asked someone if he could borrow $200. They lent him the money, he bought the suit and shoes and began to assemble his insurance business. Within a few years he had the reputation for being one of the very few honest insurance agents in the city where he lived and his business had grown to employ 25 agents.

Along the way, Timothy and his wife took some of the profit and invested in property outside of the city. They began building a retreat center—today that retreat center can accommodate nearly 300 people and is used by all kinds of people and organizations who experience the best of Christian service and African traditions. It is a unique and peaceful setting—the presence of the Lord is unmistakable.

They are now moving in the direction of supporting various initiatives for youth development. All of this is due to a well-placed $200 loan—plus the development of a heart to serve God and their neighbors. The result is two successful (profitable) businesses with employment for well over 100 people. The scope of their positive influence likely reaches a thousand more. This employment is not only a job, but also a place for individuals to develop and influence others.

Back in the U.S. a young man with a passion to help the underprivileged moved to the inner city of a major U.S. metropolis—to a slum area. He teamed up with an ex-con who had become a Christian in prison during the last of many sentences. Together, and with much help from a growing connection of supporters, they pulled off something that seemed impossible. They purchased a city block of slum tenements (for little money), created a construction company, tore the tenements down, and rebuilt housing reminiscent of a small Midwest community. Parallel to this, they created a window-washing company and a street-washing company to provide jobs for the growing community of previously down and-outers.

As they have done this they have taught and equipped people to function in a new way to be successful in raising their families—including the ability to provide for them. Their effort has caught on and is growing through family and relational networks. In fact, the learning and experience is now transitioning to another nearby metro area. The resulting multicultural communities are clearly a way to transition our difficult inner cities in the U.S. and elsewhere in the world.

The Information Age and Entrepreneurism

Glenda and Ken Cahill are innkeepers. They own and operate an Inn called "The Wildberry Lodge" outside Asheville, North Carolina. Their brochure reads, "Experience the spacious 5300 square foot lodge constructed of hand-peeled red pine logs, nestled in the Newfound Mountains of Western North Carolina. Throw away your cares and encounter a taste of heaven just minutes from Asheville."

The Cahills and their lodge are unique and it's a pleasure to spend a few days with them. How the lodge came to be is an interesting story of the convergence of the information age and the entrepreneurial spirit. Glenda is a product development manager with a packaging company and Ken is the IT manager for an amusement company that specializes in movie theater operations around the world. Both do 90% of their jobs from their 5300 square foot lodge/home on top of a mountain outside Asheville. You might say that these are their day jobs and they also do inn-keeping as a hobby.

It all started when Glenda and Ken began dreaming about living in the mountains some day and perhaps retiring there. The more they dreamed about it the more a vision of how to do it sooner, rather than later, emerged. They would build the log home of their dreams and invite guests to come, which served two purposes. First, it allowed them to live where they wanted to live—and get some help in financing the cash flow needed. Second, and ultimately more important perhaps, it would provide a flow of people for them to interact with well past their professional lives. Since they are both "people persons," they knew they would need this to eventually enjoy retirement.

A third purpose now seems to be emerging. They hire local young people (mostly women) to help them with the operations of the lodge. They have already helped a young single mom go back to school to develop skills needed to find a well-paying job in the medical field. Because of this experience they realize the potential to launch many more new-beginnings over the years to come.

This story is only one of thousands that have been made possible over the past several years as a result of the information age. The use of computers and now video-casting technologies make many things possible that used to require physical, face-to-face proximity to accomplish. I work with one company that started up a few years ago and now has several hundred people in a variety of locations around the world. Each Wednesday they have a company meeting of about 30 minutes and they connect everyone from around the world via a sophisticated video teleconferencing system.

Back to the Cottage

Back to my own story, I've gone full circle, beginning with my early years growing up with family-operated "Cottage" businesses, I segued to 30 years in the corporate world, where I replicated some of the wisdom and values from that Cottage time in a way that produced successful results. Now, I'm back to a Cottage business of my own where I have been able to help others, both corporations and cottage startups, utilize the concepts and principles I have learned as a result of this journey. So what are these core principles and concepts? The chapters that follow record what I have learned, hopefully in a way that will provide food for thought. May you begin your own quest to develop successful business environments, great places to work and good opportunities for the communities in which you reside.

Chapter 13

What is Leadership?

I believe the core values and principles we hold are foundational for our entire lives, not merely for business leadership. They anchor us in our attempts to accomplish great things. The history of business is populated with stories of individuals, groups, and communities who built and achieved great and enduring success. The common thread through all these stories—old and new—is their values and principles – values and principles that started out during the Cottage era.

But I'm disturbed that increasingly there appears to be a shifting—even crumbling—to the foundations of business.

What has changed? We still see foundational values and principles in new Cottage businesses. Some are 21st century mom & pop ventures; others survived the 20th century intact. Some, like Procter and Gamble, have retained their Cottage roots from the 19th century! All of them are organized around values and principles that hold people together and guide their business behavior. But many other companies lost those foundations in the crush of the industrial age—or have yet to find them for the first time. The result is greed, shoddy design and production, poor customer care, abusive labor practices, high turnover, shortsighted vision, employee theft, executive looting, lost fortunes . . . really too many negative repercussions to list.

The future demands that we lead a return to the Cottage, bringing that heart and those values and principles to every business we touch.

Ultimately, this means muffling the din of voices that distract leaders from what matters. Those voices generate a constant barrage of misdirection, criticism, and restriction in the name of:

1. **Speed:** We have become a point and click marketplace. We want what we want and we want it now. This drives business leaders to make decisions fast, develop products quickly, and bring them to market first. In far too many cases, speed is the father of shoddy workmanship and service.

2. **Value:** There is an ever-increasing expectation of excellent quality at ever-lower cost. In theory this balances Number 1 (Speed), but how do you accomplish it? Sure, we see progress in the development of technical goods and services, and costs are down in many cases. But there is a price to be paid and most often that cost is initially borne by stakeholders before ultimately falling hard on the shareholders who aren't wary or "smart" enough to get out early.

3. **Adaptability:** It would be easier to deal with the need for speed and value if it weren't for the simultaneous need for high flexibility and adaptability. The global nature of the marketplace generates constant change. In many business categories, no sooner do we feel like we're settling in on a product or service than a disrup-

tive innovation requires us to change quickly or face extinction.

4. Size: Businesses consolidate in order to grow and/ or control the competition. It's an "acquire or be acquired" world. The obvious downside is that attempts to merge distinct corporate cultures often have disastrous consequences for stakeholders and, eventually, shareholders.

5. Talent and teamwork: Last but not least is the need for talented people to collaborate and share knowledge like never before. But our society seems to be trending toward fragmentation rather than genuine sharing and synergy. The scramble to protect intellectual property is at an all-time high. And why not? What has the world of business done lately to encourage cooperation, loyalty and hard work? Are we not reaping what we have sown?

I'm afraid these tensions have the capacity to eat our lunch. Most business leaders have lost the heart that drives the Cottage—if they had it to begin with. These tensions seem likely to increase, but there are interesting possibilities and opportunities for those who understand and implement the values and principles of the Cottage. I've seen with my own eyes, that it is possible to have:

- enthusiastic, loyal employees, each fully involved in improving the business.
- efficient, flexible processes that deliver the highest quality at a low cost.
- consistently high quality and service (to the customer's delight).
- improved bottom line and sustained profitability over time.

140

The companies that enjoy these results are first, last and always led by people who get it, that the Cottage is not a place or an era but a state of mind and heart and values and principle-driven decision making every day.

Leadership—What is It?

Leadership can make or break the outcome of a problem, determining whether it's an opportunity for improvement or a recipe for disaster. For example, a mechanic in a plant where I worked thought a coupling for the drive system on one of our production machines wore out too fast. So he developed an improved coupling. He not only had the idea, he had the will to convince us to try it. Once he proved the concept he had to recruit help to mass-produce the coupling for the whole company (multiple machines in multiple plants needed them).

As it played out, this man's leadership saved the company hundreds of thousands of dollars a year for the life of that equipment. He had an idea, he influenced others to try it, and it improved the business results for years.

When we redesigned the work system for the Foley paper pulp mill, we drew together a cross organizational team of operators and managers to develop a conceptual design for the future. This was difficult work because operators and managers in existing operations almost never collaborate in such efforts—typically this is the work of high-level managers and consultants.

It was slow-going at first but then a machine operator who had been employed at the mill for about 15 years began to catch the significance of our aim. Seeing the potential for the group to influence the future of the business, he became a voice of reason among his peers and emerged as an unofficial leader. As a result the group developed the concept for a work system that included a number of novel ideas and most importantly would stand as their design—not something passed down to them from on high. Ownership in a project is key to adopting and implementing new concepts.

When we consider these examples of organizational leadership, it's clear that many individuals can be leaders—maybe any individual, with the right direction. This is not only possible; it is necessary if we are to be successful in a complex business world.

Every organization has both positional leaders and natural leaders. A positional leader has been awarded a role with designated responsibility for directing the actions of other people. Some folks reach positional leadership without ever being responsible (or trained) to lead; others arrive via a series of positional leadership positions. They are promoted up the ladder. In any event there is no guarantee that positional leaders know the first thing about leading. Natural leaders seem to have been born to lead. They may or may not have official standing but they recruit followers, friends and collaborators in ways that may appear quite uncanny. They know how to influence others and steer the reactions and development of concepts so others feel a part of the solution (not via manipulation, but by inspiring others to strive for excellence). Natural leaders don't necessarily even know how they do it; they just do.

Putting it Together

Putting these two types of leaders together reveals some interesting opportunities and problems. There is no question that natural leaders provide leadership. People follow them mainly because they want to. Natural leaders motivate others to action—generally without promising rewards or threatening punishment. People respond to their charisma and energy.

This is not so clear for positional leaders. Certainly we can think of many positional business leaders renowned for their leading. Benjamin Franklin, Thomas Edison, Henry

Ford, Walt Disney, Warren Buffet, Sam Walton, Jack Welch, Bill Gates, Steve Jobs . . . the list could fill a chapter by itself and, if we're honest, it would include positional leaders who led their companies to ruin (but boy did they ever lead!). We can also recall the names of positional leaders who didn't lead well; some who peaked early and never went far; and leaders who did a pretty good job at lower levels only to get lost in the executive maze.

The biggest trouble with positional leaders who don't lead is their tendency to cripple, and even kill the organizations for which they are responsible. I see three reasons why positional leaders fail:

Reason #1: They may be unwilling to change. There are, of course, many reasons why leaders might be unwilling to change their personal leadership style, but at the root of it they just don't believe anything different will produce better results than they are already getting. They may think they're already a good leader (they have the position after all), and the problem is not with them but the people who are supposed to follow them. You can see the problem with that logic, but they cannot. Or, they may believe that any attempt to involve people in decision making is misguided, i.e., they may be real Theory X thinkers—people are essentially lazy and don't want to work; management's job is to create such a tight system of control that even the laziest wage slave will produce minimally acceptable work.

Reason #2: They may be defeated by the rat race. There are positional leaders who know better and have done better in previous situations. But the rat race got to them and they don't know how to get out of it. Every time they make new vows to start doing what they know to do, the voices of the rat race cut them down to size, and they are once again reduced to being rats, just trying to win that day's race.

Reason #3: They may suffer from a lack of development. Many positional leaders know they're in trouble and even suspect they may be part of the problem (although it would be very difficult to admit that). They struggle with not knowing what good leadership looks like from the inside, much less how to achieve it. They've probably attended leadership seminars—perhaps many—and they're most likely familiar with the literature. The knowledge and information they've accumulated only confuses them further or paints a picture of something that seems desirable but unattainable. Why? Because no one developed them into fully formed leaders. They have no mentors or coaches. The burden is always and only theirs. They see that something needs fixed, but aren't sure how to resolve the issues on their own—they need guidance.

Effective leaders are willing to change because: 1) they are as humble as they are bold and 2) they understand that leadership is dynamic not static. Effective leaders rise above the rat race because they have well formed values and principles on which they thoughtfully base their vision and decision-making. Effective leaders actively seek people who can help them move from where they are toward where they need to be and they bring these people close because they understand that no one is omni-competent.

It is the scarcity of effective leaders that worries me. There are simply too many people in positions of business leadership who do not lead. We're not just talking about C-Level executives; we're also talking about supervisors on the factory floor, entrepreneurs working on startups and union leaders in local 2471.

It wouldn't be so bad if ineffective leaders were just part of an overall leadership mosaic, with others to pick up the slack. The problem is that positional leaders typically direct what goes on in the work culture. If they develop and release other leaders in the organization to do what each one is capable of doing, great things can happen. Often, however, they do just the opposite. They smother potential leaders. It's like having a 500 horsepower engine with a governor that restricts output to 10% of potential.

Of course, the natural leaders in an organization don't stop leading; they just take it underground or into side businesses or leave to join some other organization. Natural leaders will lead; its part of their nature. But they may lead in a different direction if they are not fully engaged. When this happens the weak positional leader laments, "They just don't care! Don't they realize they'll be out of a job if we don't do well?" The fact is they do care—of course they care!

What if we could draw natural leaders into the game? What if we developed our positional leaders to recognize this untapped resource and develop it? Consider the potential of an organization in which natural leaders were encouraged to develop new machine couplings or eliminate waste in the system or take the initiative to meet problems and opportunities. Endless potential.

The Opportunity

Every organization holds tremendous potential in the untapped capability of its people. Releasing that capability requires unified action toward a meaningful objective. The leader's job includes guiding the organization to define the objective and focus the action. Defining the objective depends on shared values and principles. Focusing the action depends on applying those values and principles to every dimension of the objective.

In the Foley case study two faces of leadership illuminated our way. First, Foley's positional leaders (though just a few in the beginning), adopted a set of core values that were oriented toward developing an involved, high-performance organization. Second, we worked to draw out the natural leaders inside the organization and empowered them to lead by listening to and implementing their thoughts and ideas. In a short time—less than a year—we had a cadre of positional and natural leaders throughout the organization who believed in the same values and were committed to the same objectives. The results we obtained, which were outstanding by any measure, came as a result of that total leadership.

The Bedrock

The Cottage has four primary characteristics, out of which grow a set of values and principles that are the foundation for everyone involved:

1. Everyone in the Cottage belongs to the family—literally or figuratively—and each member is in some way dependent on and responsible to all the others.
2. Each person's contribution counts; it is vital to the wellbeing of the family.
3. There is a sense that others in the family care about each other personally and are advocates for shared success.
4. Trusting relationships are forged over time, built on honesty and integrity.

These characteristics are the foundation of a set of values and principles that provide a standard for how people are to behave toward each other and toward customers, suppliers, outside partners and competitors. Certainly there is variation from Cottage to Cottage but here's an inventory of **Cottage Values** (from Chapter 3):

- Knowing what we stand for
- Knowing where we are going
- Honesty and integrity
- Valuing each individual
- Teamwork

- Planning
- Continual learning and improvement

When leaders help organizations live out these values, they get a tremendous response. This kind of leadership causes average people to pull together in ways that produce extraordinary business results. It's not a trick. It's not the flavor of the month. It's not about paying lip service or employing motivational jargon. It's about principle-driven action to engage everyone in the organization to his or her greatest capacity.

The Target: The Work of Leadership
Here, in a nutshell, is the work of Cottage Leadership:
1. **Determine Purpose and Direction.** Leaders must help the organization understand and be guided by answers to two questions: What are we here for, and where are we going? It is up to leaders to determine the answers to these questions and help the organization understand them and become aligned with them.
2. **Establish Principles.** It is a leader's responsibility to set behavior standards by establishing guiding principles and assuring that each member of the organization understands and follows them. Leaders must model these principles in their day-to-day behavior and lead the organization in regular assessments and course corrections.
3. **Develop a Planning System.** Leaders must assure the development of an up-to-date plan with clear objectives, strategies, and tactics. To the extent possible each member of the organization should be involved in developing the portion of the plan that applies to his or her area of responsibility. Leaders engage stakeholders to develop systems that measure and generate accurate information on the work process

and end results to facilitate continuous improvement in the organizational effort.

4. **Develop the People.** Leaders must assure that each member understands his or her role in the plan and receives regular feedback on necessary adjustments to continue personal development. Work is designed to enhance the growth and effectiveness of individuals and interdependent teams, including technical, interpersonal, leadership and coaching skills.

5. **Develop the Process.** All business systems have a process, i.e. all of the technical requirements needed to bring a product or service to market. It is the leader's responsibility to understand what customers expect and assure that effective systems arc in place to develop and maintain the process. These systems include equipment reliability, process consistency, supply chain management, and continuous improvement or optimization.

Not to belabor the point but, if you're like most businesspeople, there's a good chance you read the passage above thinking in positional leadership terms. So, please, skim it again thinking in terms of total shared leadership.

Leadership Skills, Abilities and Characteristics

If these five requirements represent the work of leadership, then what are the skills, abilities, and characteristics needed to do this work? The list of possibilities is lengthy, ranging from traditional business management, planning, and decision-making skills to the technical skills prompted by emerging technologies.

Over the years I have noted a collection of core characteristics and skills that are necessary to do the work of leadership.

1. **Heart and Personal Character.** Everything is predicated on these elements. Effective leaders are not only consistent in their application of a set of core values and principles, but they have a passion for them. They uphold a standard of excellence in all things. They are always truthful, maintain confidences, do what they say they will do, and admit when they can't.

2. **Respect for each individual** is contained in the above. If a leader possesses the heart and personal characteristics needed, he or she is well on the way to involving people in the organization. A person who has respect for the individual genuinely cares about people, starts relationships in the trust mode, and thinks in terms of "Theory Y" (people want to participate and make a contribution).

3. **Motivating and developing others** follow next. This is the coaching characteristic. Effective leaders have the ability to create a climate in which people want to do their best because they are making important contributions. Such leaders assure that individuals see themselves as others see them, that they have integrated career and life goals along with a development plan to achieve those goals.

4. **Building effective teams** is next. Effective leaders develop the ability to coach individuals into teams that become "fully functioning" and tend to be far more productive because they are prepared to handle their collective responsibilities with minimal outside help.

5. **Communication skill** is critical at every phase. The effective leader is an active, attentive listener and has the patience to hear people out. He or she makes sure others have the information they need to accomplish their work and build their personal capacity.

6. **The ability and willingness to learn** flows through everything. Without this characteristic leaders get stuck in "that is the way we have always done it" and cease leading. This characteristic implies a tenacious desire for continual development and growth.

7. **Courage** underpins it all. It is one of the personal character traits necessary for not only entering any new venture, but being tenacious to continue when trials surface. Effective leaders don't hold back on anything that needs to be said or done. They face up to problems and deal with them appropriately, and they take appropriate risks.

Leaders who manifest these skills, abilities, and characteristics are respected, valued, and followed in the workplace.

I think it is interesting that none of these have to do with technical, financial, or other business skills. It is also interesting to note that most of the formal training received by positional leaders has been focused on technical, financial, and other business skills. It is no wonder so few leaders truly lead—they're simply functioning the way they were trained.

This is not to say that technical, financial, and other business skills are unimportant. On the contrary, at the level of executive leadership, they should be givens. But by themselves, they are related to effective organizational leadership as the capacity to read music is related to playing concert piano.

When leaders develop these skills, abilities and characteristics, they begin to draw people into the game and the capability of the organization is multiplied as every member develops skills, abilities and characteristics far exceeding what can be commanded and controlled solely by positional leaders.

Chapter 14

The Aspects of Leadership

Aquest to better understand the difference between the management of the industrial age and the leadership needed for the future began to emerge in the 1980s. For years the word we used wasn't "leadership," it was "management." How to make management more people-oriented has created in-depth research, dialogue, and business modules.

In the 1980s the discussion seemed to turn into a debate between leadership (concern for people) and management (concern for process) as if there was now some sort of tension between the two. Further, at least in some discussions I participated in, leadership became considered as good and management bad—people were labeled as big L/little m or big M/little l and so forth.

I kind of liked it because I was labeled as Big L/little m, based on the direction my company was headed at the time. But, the big M/little l's made good points regarding the need to be organized, to have a plan, to have some system for how things should be done—those things didn't need to be so extreme that it wore down organizations in bureaucracy. That made sense to me also!

I came to understand for the first time where leadership and management came from. What I mean is you can see leadership throughout history. The story of Nehemiah in the Old Testament Bible is an excellent story of leadership. More recently the stories of leaders like George Washington, Abraham Lincoln and Ronald Reagan are wonderful examples of leadership. In these stories there are aspects of "managing" present. I doubt any leader ever accomplished much without having a plan, being organized, having a few necessary systems and so forth.

However, it was pointed out to me that management doesn't really show up historically very much until the Industrial Revolution. It was here that management became necessary in a new, big time way. With the advent of factories and mass production came "workforces" made up of people with rural, uneducated backgrounds along with waves of new immigrants who typically spoke a different language.

Another factor of the time was the previously mentioned theory developed by Frederick Taylor, expressed in his book, *Scientific Management*. This book outlined an approach to manage the new workforce phenomenon. It was a highly organized system and became the theory that people like Henry Ford put into practice in his automobile factories. No doubt, there was a need for some of this; but, as we now know, it became excessive and eventually produced organizations that were so stuck in their structured ways they couldn't adapt easily to the effects of globalization that have occurred in recent years and continue to evolve.

The term "management" became the more used term—as opposed to "leadership." It represented not only the tasks of managing but also the hierarchical levels needed to keep everything in control. It was not unusual in a large organization to have over ten levels of management, each watching the levels below, making sure they were doing what they were supposed to be doing. After hundreds of years of doing business out of a family operated Cottage, in a few short years it was like management came in and pushed out leadership. I know this isn't totally true, there have been examples of good leadership; but, by and large, we do seem to have lost something along the way, in the name of progress.

The point of sharing these concepts is to share the journey that developed my point of view regarding leadership and organizations. These concepts clearly added to my understanding, and probably adjusted several viewpoints. This (along with early experiences), formed my worldview. Out of that came a strong desire to focus on the people part of the business equation because I came to believe that was where the leverage and opportunity resided. In a word, I had developed a heart for people and that would be my leadership focus for the rest of my life.

Your journey may be different, but your quest should be to focus your energy on the right thing. If it isn't people, then for goodness sake, don't focus on that. Maybe its technology, or finances; maybe you're destined to be a marketing whiz—it's whatever you have a heart for. You can't just pick up a book and figure it out, you will need to take a journey, learn what your worldview is, add to it through experiences, learn new concepts, etc. Let that guide your heart.

The book *E-myth* by Michael Gerber (Harper Business) provides an excellent rationale for why we need management to somehow coexist with leadership. The author consulted for years with thousands of small companies, many of them startup companies. He makes this observation: Of all startups, 80% fail in the first 5 years and of those that succeed, 80% fail in the second 5 years. He goes on the say that the primary reason for this is the failure of the founding leader to provide a more organized, systematic approach for operation at the point where it becomes too big for him/her to personally handle. In other words, the lack of "management" is what sinks many startup companies.

This is an interesting conundrum, is it not? On one hand we have big corporations sinking under the weight of management, and on the other, startup companies failing from the lack of it. How can we make sense out of this?

The model we used in Chapter 7, **The 4 P's**, also works well to describe the aspects of leadership. It includes: managing (utilizing planning and practical skills to determine a course to follow), and the more typically thought of leadership characteristics (envisioning, role modeling, and coaching).

The Aspects of Leadership

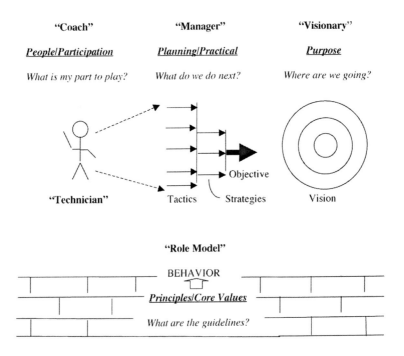

Principles—The Role Model

An interesting reality about organizations is that they tend to reflect the values of the leaders. This can be a good thing or a really bad thing, but it is almost always true. The only situation in which it may not be true is when the leader is there for too short of a time to make an impact. Because of this reality a leader must carefully consider what kind of role model they are and the extent to which they portray the character needed by the organization overall to be successful. Obviously, this will have much to do with the trustworthiness of the organization as well as its collective ability to deliver successful results. Questions regarding integrity and honesty are always present for those the enterprise serves—we all know that. What we may not be as aware of is the degree to which this is influenced by the behavior (the outward result of core values and principles) of the leader.

Note: the model is intentionally drawn to indicate Principles as being foundational to the other aspects. It could be debated whether Principles or Purpose come first—in reality they seem to work together as a "beginning" with "Purpose" describing the destination and "Principles" describing the behavior guidelines for the journey.

Because Principles/Core Values are foundational it is necessary that all leaders in an enterprise adopt them and propagate them. This starts with the "senior leader" but it's vitally important that it become true for the overall leadership, as well. The organizational behavior of the organization will adopt these principles and core values when this is true. When it is not true— i.e., the leaders are fragmented regarding principles/core values—then the organization will be likewise fragmented and dysfunctional to some degree.

Purpose—The Visionary

Not much of anything can ever happen without someone "seeing" an opportunity and acting on it in a way that creates movement. And if there are other people involved they must be enrolled in a way that causes them to want to go along. People in any organization have a basic question

155

of their leaders, "where are we going?" If that question is answered with a somewhat clear picture of the future and if that future seems like an interesting and valuable place to go, then the people will likely want to go there. If this is missed, with the leader's expectation that, "they will do it because I pay them; therefore, I don't need to explain where I want to go," the likely result is compliance—but no commitment. Without commitment it is probable that less than half of the capability of the organization will be realized, often the difference between success and failure.

Planning/Practical—The Manager

As Purpose describes the destination and Principles describe the guidelines for the journey, Planning is the leadership aspect that describes how to move forward—the roadmap. It includes organization, planning and implementation of the plan. The manager leader has both practical understanding of what needs to be done along with a capability to organize it all.

Once the people being led understand where they are going and the guidelines for the journey they have more specific questions, "how will we go?" or "what is the route?" Underlying these questions is another very specific question of the leader, "do you have the capability to lead us to this destination?" If this is not clear then even though the destination sounds good the people are likely to be reluctant to go; conversely, if it is clear that there is a route and the leader is capable then the desire to be involved is enhanced even further.

People—Technician

We have referred to "the people" as if they are just some sort of blob. They aren't, of course—they and their role is a very important leadership aspect. The term I find most useful is "Technician." It fits with "knowledge worker," a term coined by Peter Drucker. Technician is also a term Gerber uses in his book *E-myth*. I first encountered the term "technician" when working with Procter and Gamble, which for them was an intentional departure from words like "worker, employee, laborer" used in the industrial era. P & G not only wanted to call them something different, they wanted them to assume a leadership role in the effort to achieve the objective.

The degree to which technicians are involved in the strategic thinking and planning aspects of the company has much to do with gaining their commitment, and that commitment has everything to do with the final result. Also, there is always a great deal of leadership potential amongst technicians and if that potential can be understood and utilized it can boost the overall capability of the leadership of the enterprise.

Participation—The Coach

Assuming that the technicians in the organization understand and like the destination and the plan for the journey, and they understand and accept the principles/guidelines for the journey, there is one more question: "How can I get into the game," or "What part will I play?" The leader's role at this point is that of a coach—the coach develops the players (both individually and organizationally) and gets them into the game.

Obviously, just like the coach of a sports team, this is much more than just assigning the players to a position. There is also the need of a game plan that connect the players with the plan to move forward. This game plan includes personal development as well as team development and it must be dynamic; i.e., able to adjust to the ever-changing landscape of the world economic situation.

Integrating the Leadership Aspects:

Every day, a leader will draw on all of the above aspects in various degrees depending on the situation. Typically, there are tactical things that must be executed that require the Planning/Practical aspect, but a leader also needs to create and/or perpetuate a vision for those that they lead; i.e., the Purpose aspect. Additionally, the leader must be sensitive to the members of the team to understand when they need encouragement or constructive criticism or they need the leader to jump in and work with them on something — the People/Participation aspect.

Underlying it all, the leader must always be consistent, regarding personal behavior, with the organizations Principles, core values and culture; and look for opportunities to propagate them. It is unlikely that any single leader would excel at all of these aspects and this is not the expectation of the model. Leadership, to be most successful, should be thought of as a team undertaking.

Where are the Entrepreneurs?

Actually, any of the leadership styles can also be entrepreneurial. Webster defines an entrepreneur as "a person who organizes and manages an enterprise, especially a business, usually with considerable initiative and risk." A leader is defined as "one who goes before to show the way, to influence, induce or cause." So it could be said that an entrepreneur is a leader who goes before to organize and manage an enterprise, especially a business, usually with considerable initiative and risk.

Peter Drucker said, "Entrepreneurs *innovate*, innovation is the specific tool of entrepreneurship."

A further definition from the Harvard Business School is that entrepreneurship is "the pursuit of opportunity beyond the resources you currently control." In other words, to be considered "entrepreneurial" one must stretch beyond the current understanding and knowledge of things and into the unknown—they must think and act outside of the box.

If the above statement that an entrepreneur is a leader is correct, then it follows that each style of leadership could be entrepreneurial. It would not follow, however, that each leader is entrepreneurial.

Practically, as we look around, we see individuals who seem to fit the Entrepreneurial mold suggested by these definitions—but we don't see a lot of them. The definitions imply a high level of passion (heart) for whatever it is the individual is trying to create or change, an intuitive ability to see possibilities for innovation that others miss, and a high tolerance for uncertainty and risk – they are willing to take chances *before* any assurance of success.

Such individuals seem to be rare in our present cultures of big business, big organizational thinking, rules, procedures, and a general lack of patience for the really creative person who may appear a little weird.

But, as mentioned earlier, the landscape is different today. It's the Information Age and we are seeing a return to individual thinking, the "knowledge worker," to again quote Drucker— and small teams that are often spread around the globe, meeting through electronic channels of various forms, and many emerging forms for tapping individual creativity. (My previous company, Procter and Gamble, now receives roughly 50% of the innovative ideas they use to create new products—or product upgrades—from individuals not employed by the company).

All of this is very interesting—it's like a return to something that is meant to be. If we are made in God's image then perhaps we are to be more creative and entrepreneurial, not less. How is all of this to work? What makes one an entrepreneur—a few college courses? In light of the fact that something like 80% of new startup businesses fail it seems that more must be understood than the material in a few college courses, which at best would provide some beginning knowledge and possibly initiate some of the skills needed. In addition, what other help, support, and skills are needed? What character traits are necessary? How does one get started? Is there a need for apprenticeship? It's obvious, based on what we see of successful business models, that entrepreneurs bring something more to the table than excellent book learning.

Unpacking Entrepreneurism Myths

Michael Gerber, in his book *E-myth*, states that the belief that entrepreneurs start up companies is a myth. The truth, he says, is that technicians start up most companies. Technicians are craftsmen with a good idea and decide to start a business to deliver that idea on a broader basis. Whether or not the technician is an entrepreneur is not particularly important (a case can certainly be made that he/she is).

Some other myths (taken from an article entitled *Global Heroes* by Adrian Wooldridge, printed in the March 12, 2009 issue of *The Economist*), provide additional insight regarding entrepreneurism — what it is and what it isn't.

Myth	Truth
1. Entrepreneurs are "orphans and outcasts"	Entrepreneurship, like all business is a social activity
2. Entrepreneurs are just out of short trousers (ie, under 25)	The number of founders over 50 was twice as large as those under 25
3. Entrepreneurship is driven mainly by venture capital	Money for the vast majority comes from the "three Fs" — friends, fools, family

160

4. To succeed, entrepreneurs must produce world-changing new products	Some of the most successful concentrate on processes rather than products
5. Entrepreneurship cannot flourish in big companies	Many large companies are very entrepreneurial and sponsor efforts both internally and externally

In the same article the author shares the data that between 1996 and 2004 an average of 550,000 small companies were created every *month*! Separately, there is an estimate of 20 million "companies of one" in the United States. This is interesting because it suggests that the entrepreneurial spirit is alive and well in the U.S.—and seems to be growing.

Add to this the point made earlier that half of the students enrolled in U.S. colleges do not want to work for someone else—they want to start their own business as a means of support. This could lead to the startup number quoted above becoming much larger. However, if everything else stays the same, there is no reason to believe that the success rate will improve (Additional college curriculum not withstanding).

The Characteristics of an Entrepreneur

With the above in mind perhaps we can formulate a set of characteristics that would be helpful in the quest to understand what makes an entrepreneur:

1. Heart: A passion to make a difference
2. Personal Character: Integrity, humility
3. Discernment/intuition: The ability to see beyond the obvious and make good choices
4. Concept organization: Making sense out of disorganized, confusing information

5. Courage: Tolerance for risk and uncertainty, perseverance
6. Collaboration: Embracing the need for help, finding
   it, and effectively utilizing it

Note that there is no mention of business skills, financial skills, technical skills, development of people skills,
etc. This is not meant to suggest that these things are unimportant; rather it is to suggest that the above represents a
platform upon which these other skills can be built.

In the chapters that follow we clarify four important features necessary to successful leadership:
1. The heart and character needed for success
2. Learning to lead—how to do it and how to help others
3. Building an effective and successful team, organization and culture
4. The primary leadership skill: Communication

Chapter 15

The Heart and Character of a Leader

∝৯ ৶৵

In the mid-1990s the founder/owner of what is now a very successful "information age" company was coming to grips with success in his entrepreneurial efforts. His ideas of how to leverage the intellectual capital he possessed began to bear fruit and he, for the first time, had a really good problem—how to support the growth that started to exceed his personal ability to keep up with demands.

The entrepreneur hired his first employee and entered into the realm of leading and managing an organization. It was not his first experience with an organization—he had been a part of a large one before starting his business and had some idea of what not to do, but wasn't at all confident what to do to ensure a successful outcome.

He did know and believe a couple of concepts, however. First, he believed there were certain elements about doing business that were important and should never be compromised; like being absolutely trustworthy. A customer (or anyone, for that matter) would never, ever have to wonder if he could be trusted to do the right thing. Another notion he held to was that he would always prefer the needs of the client (or others) over his own, even if it meant sacrificing something himself in order to accomplish it.

As he hired his first person he determined to always find the best person possible—that meant not only smart people with the capability to learn, but also people who would fit in well with his core values. He didn't know much about how to manage people or how to develop them but he believed if he hired wisely and made sure the culture he had begun was maintained (or even improved), then the rest of it would work out okay.

As time progresses and the company has grown, the entrepreneur hasn't wavered on these ideals. He follows them to this day, and expects the rest of the team to adhere to these same values. Currently the company doesn't need to do much marketing because they are well known in their area of expertise as the company to do business with. They have a good reputation because they are excellent in what they do—both the business process part and the relationship (people) part. If they make a mistake (and they don't make many) they make it right. Their service is stellar and exceeds the expectations of their clients as well as new company staff. In the entrepreneur's words, they function according to "multiple bottom lines," 1) the profit bottom line, 2) the customer service bottom line, 3) the wellbeing of their community bottom line, and 4) the success and wellbeing of each member of the organization bottom line.

All of this has created a company that is thriving and will continue to thrive—the objective of business leaders everywhere. This is hard to imagine when they literally, at times, subjugate profit to the other bottom lines they pay attention to. But, it seems that this makes them *so* effective and desirable as a supplier of their product that, in actuality, it causes them to leap over the competition.

I contrast this with other entrepreneurial efforts I have observed. In one case the owner was already a wealthy man when he purchased the business that he later brought me in for a consultation. My task was to help the leaders develop an approach to make the company more competitive in their industry. They were losing ground. Their product quality was inconsistent and the margin of profit had decreased due to competitive pressure. This made it hard to charge their customary prices.

The owner thought it might have something to do with the people side of the equation and it became quickly apparent he was right. The workers were paid relatively low wages and received very little benefits. As a result there was no incentive to go the extra mile. Instead, workers did the minimum necessary to keep their jobs. Few were faithful to work attendance. This high absenteeism rate combined with and an extremely high turnover rate (about a third of the organization left and had to be replaced every year), resulted in a need for more people on the payroll than necessary, just to be sure enough would be at work on any given day to make the product and ship it to customers.

One of the main reasons they brought me in was to deal with these issues because their general manager had resigned a couple of weeks earlier. They were missing their chief problem solver/decision maker and couldn't diagnose the problems and brainstorm potential solutions. As you can probably imagine it really wasn't that difficult to figure out, but they were blind to see it. The business needed a better policy and approach to managing workers. They needed to improve pay and benefits as well as the working relation-ship across the organization to motivate workers with better incentives.

We worked out a plan and presented it to the owner. To justify the increase in pay and benefits, we had to show the owner a good return on his investment in terms of improved quality, production consistency and ultimately, but not for a year or two, a likelihood that the organization would be able to operate at a much lower number of people. In our proposal we carefully stated that decreasing the workforce should happen only as normal attrition allowed, otherwise the improved morale we expected to achieve would be destroyed.

I also helped the owner recruit a new general manager—a person I thought would implement this plan well. We involved him in developing the final stage of the proposal and together we presented it to the owner. The owner appeared impressed with what we shared but was not particularly forthcoming in what action he would take with our proposal. It was more "Thank you, let me have some time to consider these recommendations and then I'll let you know how I will support them."

Later, he met with me alone and asked if I thought I needed to be part of the effort any longer, given the fact that there was now a new general manager and I had completed the analysis and planning for what needed done. I was only slightly surprised by his abruptness. Over the course of time I had been involved with this man I noticed he was a different kind of person than I had been used to in much of my career. He was very independent in his thinking and at times could be abrasive with people who didn't perform to the level of his expectations. I also realized that the condition I found the business in was probably, in many ways, due to his leadership (or lack thereof).

So I went my way and became involved in other things. I didn't think much about my time with this owner and his business until, about 6 months later, I received a call from the general manager I helped them recruit. He was now the ex-general manager! He told me that regarding our proposed plan to improve the business, the owner especially took note of the possibility to reduce the staffing level and ignored the rest. The general manager argued the point—trying to impress on the owner that reducing staff before accomplishing several other elements of the proposal would only exacerbate the already bad situation. But the owner would have none of it, said he was convinced that the lower number would work as long as there was a general manager strong enough to make it work. This was the final straw in a toxic working relationship, which motivated the general manager to leave.

To this day I am convinced the business could have been quite successful had the owner been willing to listen. As it turned out I suspect that he continued to run through general managers. Perhaps some did it his way for a time until they couldn't stand it anymore—his way being to run it like a "sweat shop" and milk it for all it was worth until it could no longer be competitive at all—then shut the doors!

How can two responsible people be so different? How can one be so oriented to the importance of people and another so opposed? Where do attitudes and beliefs like these come from?

Certainly, these two illustrations are extremes of a spectrum and there are many more illustrations of leaders across that spectrum. What this experience and experience with others tell me is that the heart of leadership begins in the heart of the leader.

Personal Experience

Some years ago my company decided to do some research in an attempt to understand what the key elements are for achieving organizational excellence. A couple of my colleagues were tasked with the project and they spent about a year traveling all over the world talking to people who would have a point of view on the subject: business leaders, teachers, government officials, etc. They gleaned a vast amount of information, which they distilled down to themes to isolate key elements.

The element that very clearly stood out as #1 was leadership. Organizational excellence starts with leadership and it continues with leadership. This really comes as no surprise when you consider any variety of organizational situations that are successful and those that are not. It would be hard to think of any other element that would impact a situation as greatly as the leadership element—starting with the primary leader, the final decision maker, the one where the buck stops.

Although it may begin with this final decision-maker leader, it doesn't continue without moving from an individual leader "leading" to "leadership," which is the collection of leadership capabilities coming from all of the leaders in an organization. This can be a consistent focused approach, which brings clarity to the organization for the direction and style of the endeavor, or it can be highly dysfunctional because of no common value system or common understanding of direction and how it is to be accomplished.

Obviously, we want functional leadership, not dysfunctional—but how do we get it? If functional leadership is at the heart of excellent organizations, and if functional leadership somehow begins with a single leader (the owner, the founder, the general manager, etc.), then what is at the root of that person's ability to be like the young entrepreneur, as opposed to the greedy owner?

Going back to the story of the successful entrepreneur—I have heard him describe the essentials involved in the development of his worldview and how it has affected his beliefs regarding people. In a word, he has a "heart" for people and as a result he thinks of business as having multiple bottom lines—employees, community, financial, etc. Contrast that to the owner of the other story, who didn't have a heart for the people. Instead his interest (his heart) was focused on one bottom line—profit (ultimately the extent to which he would profit personally).

So the **heart of leadership** begins with the **heart of the leader**. Truly, whatever happens organizationally, whether it becomes excellent and well-skilled at delivering the business objective or is dysfunctional and unable to be effective to do anything of significant importance, it is very dependent on what the primary leader (the "where the buck stops" leader) believes in his/her heart of hearts regarding the value and importance of people.

Recently, I have been involved with a young leader in a large manufacturing organization. He has a degree in engineering and came to the business world with an attitude that "people are a means to an end" (his words). After some bumpy experiences—one in which he was removed from the leadership role—he began to wrestle with what he was doing wrong.

At that same point a couple of older leaders, who had the "heart" part right, began to mentor him. They provided feedback and ideas that helped him begin to connect the dots and he began to understand that people are much more than means to an end. He began to see them as unique individuals with unique abilities and skills. He realized that they, like him, wanted to do well and be able to provide for their families. He became aware of their struggles as well as their hopes, and found himself wanting to be helpful to them. When he saw them, his mind's eye imagined the faces of their families. He came to know the names of their children and what they were trying to achieve in life. In a word, his "heart" changed!

Today, the people who work for him have high regard for him and to a person they say, "He's the best boss I've ever had." His department isn't perfect but it's steadily improving and ultimately it will be a role model for other departments and leaders—a catalyst that will produce excellence for the company overall.

Isn't this what we aspire to? Don't we all want this kind of legacy? The tools and approaches are important—but we have to start with some heart issues. Do we view people as a necessary evil, a means to an end; or do we view them as a precious provision, each uniquely created by a loving God, ready to do something of lasting importance?

Unpacking the Heart

Years ago I was exposed to some concepts that helped me in the formation of a worldview that connected what I had seen in my "Cottage" growing up years and my new industrial environment. The first one provided a way to help young managers think about the difference between concern for people and concern for production. It was called "the management grid." (It is interesting that it wasn't called the leadership grid, but in 1968 management was more popular than leadership regarding organizational guidance):

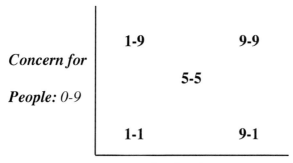

Concern for Production: 0-9

The grid contrasts "concern for people" with "concern for production" (or the business process). The various points indicated on the grid are:

    1-1: basically not involved

    9-1: Authoritarian style of managing (control and direct)

    1-9: Country club style (do whatever you like)

5-5: Compromise (middle of the road)
9-9: Team leadership (balanced, people fully involved and committed)

Of course the idea of the grid is to cause thinking beyond the typical 9-1 style that had become prevalent as the industrial age developed. It was quickly understood that a 9-9 style is the best one for bringing all of the capability and potential capability into play.

At about the same time I was exposed to theories, mentioned earlier, postulated by Frederick Taylor - Scientific Management, and Douglas McGregor - Theory X and Theory Y. Theory X is the management belief that workers are basically lazy, they don't want to work and they have to be closely managed to assure that they do what they are supposed to do.

Actually, this sounds a lot like Scientific Management - Taylor's idea was that management would have to construct a system of rules and procedures so thorough that a worker wouldn't have to think about anything, just come to work and do a certain set of tasks every day. He went on to suggest that this would cause workers to be happy and well adjusted in their work.

Certainly we know that the opposite is true—workers became disgruntled and unhappy as a result of industrial age systems that basically forced them to "check their brains at the gate" as they entered the workplace.

The other theory that McGregor postulated was Theory Y: that workers are not lazy, they want to work, make a difference and be appreciated for their work. It didn't take long for me to latch on to this way of thinking because it was how I wanted to be treated. Also, in the family business in which I grew up, my father and grandfather treated the people who worked for them as equals and counted on their full participation.

I recall that in those early years as a young manager it was suggested that if you were a Theory X believer you probably should not try to lead a team of people—it would only frustrate the team members and they in turn would frustrate you because they really wouldn't be a very good team. If you really wanted to lead people and develop good teamwork you must be a Theory Y believer. If you really aspired to the 9-9 style on the management grid you would never reach it unless you were a Theory Y believer.

The combination of these ideas along with my cottage background formed a worldview from which I developed values that were extremely important in my quest to be a leader and then to coach and develop other aspiring leaders.

Character •

I invited a longtime friend and colleague to help me do a workshop with one of my clients on the subject of developing and leading teams. This is an area where he excels, and now in his 60s, he is in the process of passing this knowledge along to others.

The workshop was to take two days but Bob went in a day early to meet each attendee to get to know them. The second and third days he did the workshop and it was very successful in terms of achieving interaction and discussion from all who attended. His last day there, Bob spent time with the participants in their work areas. The purpose of this time was to answer any lingering questions from the workshop and also help them begin to implement some of the workshop ideas.

As we left we had the sense that the whole effort had gone well but it wasn't until my next visit that I realized how much. The workshop had been conducted for the leaders in one of the departments and in short time all of the departments had heard about it and wanted to get some time with

Bob. I asked what it was about Bob that caused him to be so popular so quickly. Here is what I heard:

- Bob has a love for the "game"
- He believes what he is talking about
- He's been there, done that
- He helped us individually

I've known Bob for over 30 years and his character was fairly well formed when I met him, but over the years he has made a point to continue developing it—especially in terms of understanding others and how he can best meet their needs. He is a coach to put it simply. In another life he might well have been a basketball coach—basketball is a passion of his.

Lou Holtz, the legendary coach of the national championship Notre Dame football team a few years back, says players have three questions of their coaches or leaders:

- Can I trust you?
- Are you committed to excellence?
- Do you care about me?

I think those questions provide profound insight into the subject of leadership and what really counts in the hearts and minds of the people we lead/coach. In less than a week, Bob answered these three questions for the players/young leaders he coached. There is no doubt in my mind that if Bob continued as their coach he would have a championship team in short order.

Why is this so? Why is it that some individuals have this capability and others don't? I believe it goes back to the heart idea. Bob has a heart for the game and it seems to somehow transcend all of the warts that he also has (we all have warts, so to speak, don't we?). No great coach or leader is perfect—but for the truly great ones, there is something that seems to override the imperfections. I think it has everything to do with the phrase, "he has a 'heart' for the game!"

But what does this mean? Are we talking about the physical heart—that organ that pumps blood to our bodies? Well, sort of. As our physical heart is central to our lives, leadership is central to the life of an organization and the leader's heart is central to that leadership. But I think the analogy to the physical heart ends there, and what helps me is to think in terms of *character* as the best way to understand the heart of a leader.

Defining Character:

The dictionary has several definitions of the word character. Here are a few:

- The features and traits that form the individual nature of a person
- Moral or ethical quality; Qualities of honesty, fortitude, integrity, etc
- An odd, eccentric, or unusual person
- A person represented in a drama, story; a role, as in a play or film
- A symbol, used in a system of writing

The various faces of the word "character" could represent a variety of leadership styles, ranging from one who is not really leading but rather a symbol, put in a position to represent something (a figurehead). They follow the company or organizational line and take care not to veer from it.

Some leaders actually do play a role of sorts, like an actor. And then there are those eccentric leaders who play their own roles—but it's still like a role in a play—about them!

Then there are the leaders who are strongly marked by traits that individualize them as one worth following. These character traits makes it possible and actually easy to do so—others want to go where they are going and do what they are doing. The leader's character produces commitment, instead of mere compliance. This is the difference between *good* and *great*!

Another way to think about character development is a verse I've paraphrased from Romans 5:4, "Dealing with hardships leads to perseverance which ultimately leads to character and hope."

So if character are those features and traits that mark us—not physical things but the things within that are behind the behavior that can be seen—and if the verse is true that dealing with the issues of life, the ups and downs, can produce perseverance that leads to character and hope, then we can summarize by saying character begins with the inherent traits we are born with and develops over time as we grow into maturity. Further, the very things we want to avoid, such as hardship and suffering, are actually part of the growth equation and even necessary for our character to fully form.

If, when we meet someone of strong character—able to relate well with others, trustworthy, empathetic, wise, etc.—and we talk with them about his or her life journey we can often spot some of the things that brought about this strongly positive character.

For some it was growing up in a large family where Mom and Dad lovingly but surely expected all to pitch in and share the load.

For another, it was participating in a war where life or death was a function of trusting and counting on the person next to you.

For still another, it was a personal tragedy like the death of a loved one.

For most of us, it is just the normal ups and downs of life—times of exultation and times of frustration and disappointment.

The common thread for all of these stories is that the individual faced each situation and persevered. They did not cut and run or find a way to cheat their way around the obstacle in their path. They stayed true to certain moral and ethical standards as they did their best. In the end that perseverance defined who they were; that is, their character.

This produces the character we admire and forms the foundation from which we can be exceptional as leaders (coaches) in our response to the 3 questions:

- Can I trust you?
- Are you committed to excellence?
- Do you care about me?

For the past few years I've been involved as a coach for an emerging leader who didn't believe he was cut out to lead. Bruce developed a very high level of expertise in his profession by the time I met him in his late 30s. It was so high that others noticed and sought him out for advice—advice he was happy to provide, because he truly cared for others (a trait with which he grew up).

But this advice-giving expanded and the organization he is a part of wanted him to be the leader of the group. He did this while saying, "I don't know how to do this and I have never been a leader." Still, the company grew and before long Bruce was responsible as a leader of leaders—kind of the head coach for his area of involvement. He still thought he wasn't the best one for the role because he had never been a leader.

This is not unusual in organizations, is it? The one of high expertise and ability becomes the leader —but there is no formal training or development approach to help them do it. Many fail as a result and may even fall below where they were when the whole leadership thing came up in the first place.

Bruce felt that way. He wondered if he could ever be successful now and truthfully, he wasn't doing that great as a leader. Plus he felt he wasn't doing much in the areas in which he excelled—because of all the time required to help others. But Bruce wasn't about to cut and run. He made up his mind to face it and did few important things to progress. He assessed the situation and from that created a personal development plan. One of the aspects of his development plan was mentoring support and he enlisted several people to help him implement the plan. Then he went to work on it.

Recently, he had an assessment done to see how he was doing. He asked several in his group of teams to give input. Some very positive themes emerged. Here is what they said:

- Bruce has really worked hard on developing his leadership abilities
- We trust him
- He expects excellence from himself and he expects it from us
- I know he cares about me

These themes were summarized from the verbatim comments of 10 people—there was no attempt to force them into any particular form but they do answer the 3 questions players have of their coaches very well. Bruce is well into a process of becoming a strong leader and it was due to some outstanding beginning traits—he cared about others, he had a commitment for excellence, and he was not willing to give up. Plus he exhibits a willingness to take some uncomfortable steps to build on those traits. The rest was a matter of doing it (repetition) with coaching support for the adjustments and refinements necessary to really get it right.

This is not the sort of thing we concentrate on learning for a time and once we learn, we possess. Rather, it is a life-long pursuit and development of the character traits that reflect the leader's heart.

The Key Elements of Successful Leadership Character

Back to the definition of character: *the features and traits that mark us*—let's discuss these key elements. The list and explanations that follow are the ones I have observed to be important in developing the kind of leadership that truly delivers the organizational commitment that we all want:

Humility

A fundamental building block for leadership character, humility (being humble), is defined as *not proud or arrogant; courteously respectful*. The Bible describes it as *considering others as more important than ourselves*. Often, humility is viewed as weak, meek, and not a part of leadership. Leadership, after all, is the courage to step out and act—right?

In the illustration provided of the young leader earlier in this chapter, a transition occurred that propelled him from being just okay as a leader to being quite successful. This transitional time developed humility in him. We may say something like, "that experience knocked some of the chips off," referring to a chip on the shoulder—just another way of describing too much focus and concern for self.

Jim Collins, in the book *Good to Great*, describes a leader of a great company as one you are probably not even aware of, because he or she spends their time and energy raising up other leaders. It's as if they have sacrificed themselves for the overall betterment of the enterprise—novel idea! Actually, not a new idea at all, but the truth is, we don't see it a lot in organizational behavior. Why not?

Is it because those who have great ability and capability eventually become the position leaders? Quite often one of the problems with people who have great ability is that they also have become very aware of just how great they are. They are very proud of themselves and find it difficult to trust others to do anything as well as they would plus, in some cases, they like the limelight on center stage. To be in the limelight they might even do unusual things to enhance it—like cheat, push others aside, not develop others to take over, etc.

The truth is, and Collins' research verifies it, these leaders (impressive though they may be), do not achieve as much organizationally as their counterparts who sacrifice their potential fame for the total success possible when all of the organization is developed and performing to its potential.

So what does humility look like for leaders of organizations? How does it actually play out? Here are some thoughts based on my observations:

It's when leaders—

- are not focused on themselves, rather they are focused on others. They see your ideas and vision and employ their abilities to *help* you in areas where you aren't as strong (as opposed to *using* you to further their objectives).
- look you in the eye and talk to you, as if you are the most important person in the room. The leader is not looking at his watch or giving off other signals that say "I've got more important things to do."
- are intra-dependent as opposed to independent.
- are more excited about your idea than theirs, in fact they would rather give you their idea and let you develop it and then applaud your effort with no mention of any involvement of their own.
- take the blame for the failures of the organization and give all the credit to the people for the successes.

- are open to input, feedback—to the point of soliciting it and helping people feel comfortable and safe in providing it.
- believe that people are more important than material things or processes. They believe that people are the solution to most issues—not the barrier.
- realize that people are God created. He loves each one and wants leaders, as well as all individuals, to do likewise.

To really step up to leadership in a way that produces the greatest effect, leaders must first examine his/her heart. Do you have the heart for what you are about to do? More importantly, are you willing to sacrifice the glory and recognition you might receive for the greater good of many becoming leaders due to your coaching and support? In other words, do you have the humility to do what needs to be done without concern of who gets the credit?

Integrity

Like humility, integrity is also a fundamental building block in the development of leadership character. The dictionary defines integrity as *the quality of possessing and steadfastly adhering to high moral principles or professional standards*. This would include always being honest and truthful, along with possessing a high degree of reliability.

When an individual talks about a leader as being a person of integrity—what they typically mean is that you can count on them to be and to do what they said they would be or do.

What does integrity look like? If you're a leader of integrity, you:

- say what you mean and mean what you say.
- are honest and truthful in all things.
- always do what you say you will do, and explain why if you can't.

- say, "I'm sorry" when you make a mistake, and then correct it.
- are willing to sacrifice for what you believe in.
- can be counted on to not repeat something told to you in confidence.
- can be counted on to never embarrass others.
- are worthy to be trusted.

The integrity of the leader is a primary building block to create trust in an organization. Without integrity, trust-building stalls out and is not likely to resume until it is reestablished. However, reestablishing integrity (or trust) once stalled out is very difficult.

Since all leaders are people and all individuals are imperfect it is reasonable to expect that no leader can be perfect regarding integrity; but, you must be ready to admit and acknowledge when you fall short. When a leader owns his or her shortcomings, the end result is that the leader actually earns even more respect. The leader's reputation for integrity grows. When there is no willingness to admit a mistake, a failure of judgment, or whatever it is, that leader loses integrity. Saying, "I was wrong, I'm sorry" is being truthful and builds integrity and consequently the character of the leader.

Wisdom

Wisdom is a combination of judgment, discernment and concept organization capability. Judgment is *the process of forming an opinion or evaluation by discerning and comparing*. Discernment is *the quality of being able to grasp and comprehend what is obscure; to see what is not evident to the average mind*. Words like discrimination, perception, penetration, insight, acumen are aspects of this trait. Another word that helps describe this trait is intuition: *quick and ready insight, the ability to know or recognize based on minimum data or analysis.* Concept organization is the *ability to make sense out of disorganized, confusing information and data.*

Great leaders have these qualities. You can see beyond the obvious. With a minimum amount of analysis you have comprehensive understanding regarding a situation. You can untangle and make sense out of confusion. People are motivated to action when a leader can size up a situation quickly and provide a needed decision, direction, or solution. Weak leaders might require much more time to come to the same conclusions. To a degree, these traits stem from a natural giftedness. That is not to say it can't be developed. Like all "emotional intelligence" learning it must be developed over time, through experience and coaching.

How does this work? It's when leaders—
- really seek to understand before being understood. You are very aware of what is going on because you ask good questions and listen to understand.
- constantly evaluate what you hear and understand, and organize it into context with other things you understand—like an ongoing analysis in which you are comparing, discerning, evaluating, and organizing.
- know what you know and what you don't know (and are honest with yourself and others about that level of knowledge).
- develop an instinct as to when to speak and when to listen more.
- continue to read the situation even as you are leading.
- make course corrections with good judgment because you continue to read the situation while processing ongoing knowledge and understanding.
- faithfully do after-action reviews to understand even further what went well and what could be improved the next time.

Courage

Courage is the "backbone" element of character. It is defined as *the ability to face danger, difficulty, uncertainty, or pain without being overcome by fear or being deflected from a chosen course of action.* Without the courage to do something, nothing can happen. This is the character trait that assimilates a concept from talk and ideas to action.

Courage is:
- the outward display of your beliefs.
- staying the course, persevering, not giving up—even when the course is uncomfortable, unpleasant, painful.
- tolerance for risk and uncertainty.
- confronting an issue which requires giving critical and sometimes unpleasant feedback to an individual (who may be defensive and difficult to communicate with).
- standing up to opposition regarding a direction you believe is right, even if it could mean the loss of your job.
- not being *overcome* by fear. It does not mean "no fear" or "fearless."

Courage with humility is strength under control. Courage with integrity is truthful and accurate. Courage with judgment and discernment assures that the right thing is being done.

Courage is the character element that causes a leader to move forward or stand up and be counted. It is the element that demonstrates to others what the leader is about—what they're made of. It is this element of a leader's behavior that others rally around. When a leader of humility, integrity, and judgment demonstrates courage by going first, ("Let's charge that hill!"), others will follow.

Collaboration

Collaboration is where two or more people work together, each making a unique contribution toward achieving a common objective. Solomon said, "two are better than one, because they have a good return for their work: if one falls down his friend can help him up. But pity the man who has no one to help him up...though one may be overpowered, two can defend themselves, and a cord of three strands is not quickly broken" Ecclesiastes 5: 9 – 12.

It is a foolish leader who tries to do it all himself/herself. Leadership is a team sport and is best done by collaborating with a few others who can add strength where you are weak and ideas outside of your box. It can be sloppy but it is the best way to assure that you aren't limiting yourself by your-self.

What does it look like? With whom do we collaborate?
- It's the people around us — mentors and coaches, peers, followers.
- People who are interested in us and willing to listen to us; who give us feedback and provide fresh perspectives and ideas.
- People who fill the gaps (no leader has it all). Ones who cover us in our weak areas.
- A safe place — a place to talk out dreams and share frustrations.
- A way to share your vision and find encouragement to go for it — at times to hear cautions to which you've been blinded.
- The team that you not only share the vision with, but also the *journey* to achieve it.

Creating a Culture of Trust

All of these character elements: Humility, Integrity, Wisdom, Courage, and Collaboration, lead to Trust. Trust is the glue that intersects all the others and holds the organization together.

When a leader's heart and character are aligned in this way it produces a principle-based center of trust that in turn results in organizational <u>commitment</u> to the overall objectives of the enterprise. This is a stark and very positive contrast to the rule-based <u>compliance</u> experienced in most industrial age companies. This commitment cannot be dictated or forced, it happens only when individuals are persuaded through the integrity of their leader's behavior, the truthfulness of their leader's words and the rightness of the cause they are being asked to join. Once this commitment is achieved, the attainment of the cause is assured.

Words from an American Leader

When the conduct of men is designed to be influenced; persuasion, kind, unassuming persuasion, should ever be adopted. It is an old and true maxim, that a "drop of honey catches more flies than a gallon of gall." So with men; if you would win a man to your cause, first convince him that you are his sincere friend. Therein is a drop of honey that catches his heart, which, say what he will, is the great high road to his reason, and which, when once gained, you will find but little trouble in convincing his judgment of the justice of your cause, if indeed that cause really be a just one.

On the contrary, assume to dictate to his judgment, or to command his action, or to mark him as one to be shunned and despised, and he will retreat within himself, close all the avenues to his head and his heart; and tho' your cause be naked truth itself...you shall no more be able to reach him, than to penetrate the hard shell of a tortoise with a rye straw.

Such is man, and so must he be understood by those who would lead him, even to his own best interest. —Abraham Lincoln, *Lincoln on Leadership*, Donald T. Phillips 1992

Chapter 16

Learning to Lead

How does an individual develop the Cottage mindset and the heart characteristics to become a leader? Why is it, of the ones who dream to become leaders, some achieve it and others never attain it?

In Chapter 5 I told the story of Nehemiah as an example of a leader drawing on the people around him to accomplish a significant result. Nehemiah's leadership made it a reality by bringing together the assets needed as well as organizing the people to rebuild the city. His story is worth repeating as an illustration of the components involved in learning to lead. It's the story of the Jews returning to Jerusalem after years of exile in Babylonia.

Jerusalem was destroyed by the Babylonians 70 years earlier and most of the people taken captive to Babylonia. The remnant left behind quickly became defeated and demoralized. During the exile in Babylonia, Nehemiah was born and eventually trained to serve the Babylonian king. Nehemiah did so well that the King gave him the role of serving his personal needs. This position gave Nehemiah the connection he needed to eventually do what no one else could do.

When Nehemiah was young, he was raised, as Jews have been raised throughout the ages, in the faith—as a believer of God and a student of God's ways as outlined in the Torah (the first 5 books of the Bible). His religious upbringing prepared his heart, and the work he did as a servant proved his character. He was given a position reserved for those highly trustworthy— cupbearer to the king. As such, he sampled the king's wine to make sure it was safe before it he served it to his employer.

How does this life experience bring us to Nehemiah rebuilding a city? He had no business training, no experience in building things, none in leading organizations. How on earth did he think he could do something nobody else had been able to do?

He had four things going for him. First, he had a tremendous passion to go to Jerusalem and do something to help his people. He was fervent—to the point of being willing to sacrifice everything if necessary. He also believed that this was something God wanted him to do. He felt a special calling (which added to the passion of course). Third, he had an ability to learn and understand situations that came from his early training, both in the ways of his own culture (Jewish), but also how to adapt to a different culture (Babylonian) and be successful. Fourth, he had the king's support, which was directly connected to the quality of the work he had done for the king—as insignificant as that work might have seemed. In many ways Nehemiah was better prepared than most entrepreneurs today starting a new business.

Nehemiah went to Jerusalem escorted by some of the king's own guard, provisioned from the king's holdings (materials for building). When he arrived he made a survey of the damage, listed what needed to be done, and cast the vision to the people. "You see the trouble we are in: Jerusalem lies in ruins, and its gates have been burned with fire; come, let us rebuild the wall of Jerusalem and we will no longer be in disgrace" (Their enemies had free access into and out of the city because the walls and gates had all been destroyed).

Nehemiah also told them about, "the gracious hand of God on Him, and what the King had said to him." The people caught the vision and were encouraged by Nehemiah's passion and the fact that he had connections beyond himself. He was not a lone wolf coming to be the hero of the day. In fact he came with the king's approval and provisions. Plus he had something else so important for a leader to have—he knew who he was and what he was about, and he wasn't about to be stopped.

They went to work. But, first they had an organizational planning meeting. Nehemiah did a very clever thing—he didn't try to figure out all of the details of what needed to be done. He recognized the people knew better than he (especially for the portions of the wall next to their house or place of business, or the synagogue in the case of the priests), so he simply and brilliantly assigned each to the portion of the wall, or the gates, that they knew the best.

There are those who believe the leader should be the one who knows the most about whatever needs to be done. The inevitable result of this is that the leader becomes a bottleneck and the effort, as well as individual thinking and innovation, bogs down.

True leadership is finding a way to release all of the individual capability in a way that produces a huge synergistic effort that can accomplish much. That's what Nehemiah did and it not only spread the responsibility to everyone in the city it also allowed Nehemiah, as the overall leader, to pay attention to issues that he otherwise might not have had the time to deal with.

By the way, the result of this entrepreneurial effort was pretty impressive—52 days from start to completion—the wall finished, the gates rebuilt, and some difficult organizational issues resolved. In fact, the community was more unified and peaceful than they had been in years, perhaps ever. Not bad for a young servant boy who became an entrepreneur-leader almost overnight.

Learning to Lead—7 aspects:

1. <u>Natural ability</u>: Some leaders seem to have an aspect of leadership skill they are born with. Raw ability to lead—such as physically being able to run fast, or a mental ability to learn, or a creative ability to make something beautiful. No one would be strong in every category and probably many of us doubt we have any natural ability.

   There is a growing understanding that leadership takes a different kind of ability than just the ability to be an engineer or a skill in financial wisdom or the knowledge to practice medicine or law—the roles we might associate with high IQ. Leadership requires some additional abilities referred to as emotional intelligence (EQ), which refers to those capabilities that allow a person to understand themselves and others and be able to relate well with other people— these are, of course, extremely important in the quest to become an effective leader.

   It isn't altogether clear the extent to which one is born with this capability versus it being developed in one's formative years. In any case it does seem clear that further development is needed for an individual's leadership ability to be most effective. Just as it takes work to polish a natural ability to run fast or sing a song or paint a picture—if the time and effort (and necessary help) isn't invested to develop leadership traits into something useful and productive it won't become so.

2. **Early Development:** The first development likely would be a result of the environment in which one grows up—especially the influence of an older person like a parent or teacher, who would recognize certain traits in a child and facilitate further development of them. Nehemiah was born into captivity. He was probably tutored by someone he respected and from whom he could learn. Like many cultures in slavery, the Jewish culture would have done all they could to preserve their ways, so whether or not parents were involved with young Nehemiah, someone was probably there to teach him.

What did they teach? They would have taught from historical writings available as well as practical life skills a young man or woman needed. Like our culture in America, the Jews of that time had a rich heritage in the form of what is now the old testament of the Bible. Stories of people like Abraham, Joseph, Moses, Joshua, David and Daniel (all excellent leaders), would have provided much for a young lad to think about—just as we learn from more recent great leaders such as Washington, Lincoln, Churchill, Martin Luther King, and Ronald Reagan.

Nehemiah would also have studied and benefited from men like Isaiah and Jeremiah—the prophets of that time who brought the Word of the Lord to the people. For example Jeremiah wrote, before Nehemiah was born, "This is what the Lord…says to all I carried into exile…'Build houses and settle down; plant gardens and eat what they produce. Marry and have sons and daughters; find wives for your sons and give your daughters in marriage, so that they too may have sons and daughters. Increase in number there; do not decrease. Also, seek the peace and prosperity of the city to which I have carried you into exile. Pray to the Lord for it because if it prospers, you too will prosper'" Jeremiah 29: 4-7 NIV.

The combination of stories about earlier leaders, who not only survived slavery but excelled to the point of becoming top leaders in those foreign cultures, probably prepared Nehemiah in terms of his worldview—and the resulting beliefs, attitudes, and assumptions that made up who he was. In Chapter 15 we talked about the *heart* and *character* of a leader—this is where the development of heart and character would have started for Nehemiah.

3. The next aspect of becoming a leader would be to **become aware of who you are,** what you believe and what you stand for, and of the world around you. This is the formation of the emotional intelligence and leadership character traits.

Many leaders are not particularly self aware, nor are they interested in how others think. They function out of their own knowledge and may lead from a position, but in reality they have no followers. Their authority comes from the position and whatever power it provides; people may do what they say to do—but only out of fear or because it is simply the more convenient way to go. There is compliance but no commitment.

In order for a leader to be able to influence others in a way that produces commitment they must first understand themselves, understand those around them and connect the two in a way that causes trust to occur: From that, commitment can be achieved.

Nehemiah grew up as a slave and developed for service to the king. As this happened someone also trained him regarding his Jewish culture and gave him a desire (a heart), to preserve that culture as well as a capability serve the king so well that he found favor. In the process he wound up with a huge amount of emotional intelligence and the character traits needed to lead.

So what are the implications of all of this? What if we don't grow up with a very good sense of who we are and the world around us? What if we have spent our formative years in a lifestyle that just didn't facilitate maturing as a leader very well?

This is a very real thing. Many in our culture today do not acquire the capabilities that Nehemiah did. They don't grow up as slaves and there isn't much focus on learning from former leaders in the way Nehemiah would have learned. How can we overcome these limitations?

The good news is that these capabilities can be developed. I have seen it in my own experience personally, and in my work with a large number of leaders and aspiring leaders over the years. Daniel Goldman's books on Emotional Intelligence, *Leadership that gets Results* and *Primal Leadership*, have corroborated this experience. (A side note: Goldman also indicates that this capability isn't picked up quickly. We can't just read a few books and learn it. I concur—it takes time and practice, based on what I've lived and observed. Emotional Intelligence comes by experiencing opportunities to perform, receive feedback, do it again and repeat this process over time. Actually, it's one of those skills that we never stop learning.)

4. **Connecting with the world around us:** The next aspect is for the potential leader to successfully connect this capability with the world around him/her.

This isn't automatic, no matter how well prepared a leader is. Discipline is required: the discipline to listen ("be quick to listen, slow to speak"), observe (what is the king's objective?) and learn (how can I help the king succeed?). Of course there may well be things the king wants to achieve that we shouldn't align ourselves with—but in Nehemiah's situation it was probably mostly house servant activity the king wanted from him. He must have done it well and cheerfully and proved himself trustworthy because he became the cupbearer. Now, that is a role we don't have today. But we do have roles which we label as "gopher" roles (Go 'fer this, go 'fer that!).

The truth is that most of us think we are above this kind of thing. Most young people would not dream of doing what Nehemiah did or what many in our own culture have done in earlier times to get started. They may be extremely sharp in many things but two traits are missing. First, humility—the attitude we develop when we really do grunt work and there is no one lower than us on the totem pole. The second attribute missing is gratefulness—that's the attitude we develop when we move from the first to the second rung in the ladder. It's still low but, oh, it's so much better than where we were!

By the time many young, aspiring leaders finish their formal educations and move into the world of work they simply expect more. They have no humility and are not grateful for much of anything. When they become part of an organization they find it very hard to connect to any extent beyond being an individual contributor—they don't understand the mechanics of trust-building or truly caring for another individual. If and when they are promoted to a leadership role it is based on their individual capability and guess what? They are lousy leaders!

So, to be an effective leader someday, one probably should start on the bottom, and learn the life lessons needed, then when it's time to connect on a larger scale, do it with a sense of humility, gratefulness and respect for those around you and for those who have gone before you.

A second important element in connecting to the world around us is that to lead one must have a *message*. What will you say, when the opportunity presents itself, that will cause others to take note? In the story of Nehemiah there were two major opportunities noted. When the king noticed that he wasn't as cheerful as normal he asked Nehemiah about it. Nehemiah's message wasn't prepared, but he was ready. The second time Nehemiah spoke his heart message was when he got to Jerusalem and needed to say something to the people to set a direction. He knew what he was there for but he took a little more time with a few others (his inner circle) to investigate the situation and prepare his message. Then, when he gave the message it was short and to the point and he connected with the people.

If we are well prepared in terms of development, have all the sensitivity in the world regarding others, but can't express what we are about and how that might be of interest to others then we still fail to be able to influence others—that is—we fail to lead. Again, a position leader can command something and people may do it out of *compliance*—but there won't be the *commitment* needed to do something truly great. So, for a leader to connect with the world around —to influence and cause those being led to be committed—the leader needs a strong message (which communicates an objective of *excellence*) coming from a character which communicates humility, integrity, courage, care, and trust. This is what people want to see in a leader, this is what they will follow and this is what they will be committed to.

5. **Teaming up:** The fifth aspect demonstrated by Nehemiah when he finally got to Jerusalem was to team up with a few others. Even after months to think about it, and the support of the king in terms of provisions and materials, Nehemiah "set out during the night with a few good men" to survey the damage and make final plans. Throughout the project to rebuild the city he maintained this connection with his team, his inner circle, as well as with the community at large. In other words, he never saw himself as being by himself. He knew he needed help to complete his plan. (Probably another thing he learned in his growing up years.)

   We tend to think in terms of the "rugged individual" when we think of strong leaders. Actually, the best leaders over time have tended to be "team players" first, and they continue to be team players no matter how high they go in terms of position.

6. **Connecting people with the process** needed to accomplish the objective: One of the more impressive aspects regarding Nehemiah's rebuilding of Jerusalem was the way in which the community was organized to do it. As you read through this portion of the story it gets a little boring because it is a listing of family units (or in some cases special groups having a common interest) and the portion of the wall or a gate for which they were responsible. The

picture you get however is a very interesting one—teams with common values and a common objective focused on the very thing needed to sustain their way of life.

Surely there would be many ways to organize this work. Why not separate out people by skill or talent and create more of a systematic way to do it with the most skilled doing the parts that required it and the least skilled doing the gopher work? That's how we did it in the industrial age—right? Well, this was before the industrial age so maybe they didn't know any better. Or, maybe they had a leader that understood human nature and what would cause a commitment beyond anything many of our industrial age leaders ever understood.

Just imagine a leader simply saying: "Ok, Smith family, how about tackling the wall next to your house—you know it better than any of us—and let us know how we can support you!" End of direction needed for the Smith family. They knew what they needed to do and they got to it.

7. **Become a "Barrier Buster":** There was one more thing that Nehemiah did along the way that provided a real positive to the process—he broke down a few barriers that were getting in the way. In fact they were potential show-stoppers and had he not addressed them, the whole effort may well have collapsed.

I imagine all of us have seen something akin to this in our experience. It could be in the form of something within our responsibility—a disgruntled, dysfunctional employee (or group of employees), or something outside like a changing market situation or government regulation. Failure to act invites disaster and the leader is the one who must act. We may not know exactly what to do, that's why an "inner circle" with a collective knowledge that is greater than our own is so important.

Personally, I have never seen an organizational setting where there wasn't a barrier of some sort—either present or forming. Usually, it is in the form of naysayers. It must be dealt with—respectfully—but it must be dealt with. The old adage, "a rotten apple will spoil the barrel" is so true.

We might be able to deal with it by reasoning with the naysayers—often they are what they are because they don't understand, or are frustrated because no one seems to be listening to them. Sometimes something as simple as that works. Listen to them, sincerely understand them and act on what you hear (hear it out, consider it, and respond back). Rarely, do barriers need to be blown away—they need to be adjusted, and helped to fit with the direction the organization needs to go to accomplish their objective.

Summary

We've discussed seven aspects involved in learning to lead:

1. <u>Natural ability</u>: we are all born with some capabilities, some of us more than others with respect to leadership. This is where it starts—it is each individual's foundation.

2. <u>Early Development</u>: What we learn and how we develop in our formative years builds on this natural ability and hopefully adds in a positive way to our potential to be a leader.

3. <u>Becoming aware of who we are</u>: Certainly this begins in our formative years but really kicks in as we reach early adulthood and being to try things. In the process of doing this we begin to see just what capability we

have to lead. From there we can focus on developing the aspects of leadership that will count the most.

4. <u>Connecting with the world around us</u>: Developing our ability to relate to others—beginning with a willingness to start in the trenches and learn who we are in relationship to others. Then develop the habits that can connect us with others and the world around us.

5. <u>Teaming up</u>: We are no stronger than the people we gather around us —our inner circle. Learning to gather people around us, to listen to them carefully, and then make use of what they offer matures our leadership abilities.

6. <u>Connecting people with the process</u>: This is the operational aspect of leadership. What is the plan of action we will follow to accomplish our objective? This was the genius of the Nehemiah story—the reason for such a success in a short period of time.

7. <u>Becoming a Barrier Buster</u>: Let the people do the work. Oversee and look for situations, issues, and problems that are not being resolved and in need of leadership help. It is critical to use good judgment as to when to get involved. Too fast and too much is micromanaging and smothering. Too little, too late can allow a problem to develop which turns out to be a disaster.

These seven aspects describe how one learns to lead. From them we can develop intentional steps and approaches to facilitate this learning.

Our objective is to develop leaders who can build individual and team capability that will consistently provide excellence, efficiency, and confidence to stakeholders. Our core belief regarding this development is that it is not learned by reading books or listening to lectures (although these

forms can be useful to create a beginning point of understanding). It is learned, forged really, by doing it.

A verse in the old testament Bible states, "Look to the
rock from which you were cut, and to the quarry from which
you were hewn", Isaiah 51:1. Everyone starts life with something inherited in terms of gifts and talents. The question is,
how will these be forged (hewn) into behaviors and skills
that allow us to be effective in the world around us?

The answer is in the natural experiences we each have,
supported by coaches and mentors who provide ongoing
feedback to help us see ourselves as others see us, and from
those observations take positive development steps that will
allow for significant results.

Chapter 17

The Inner Circle — and Beyond

∶∶

The leader's heart and character is foundational to being effective and successful as a leader whether it is to entrepreneur the start up of a new venture or to lead an existing organization and entrepreneur through innovation. In either case one must also have an inner circle.

Recently, a colleague and I were discussing what makes a leader great and our discussion turned to U.S. presidents. We both felt that Ronald Reagan was one of the great ones and I asked my colleague why he thought that.

His answer strikes me as one of the key elements for a leader to become truly great. He said, "Reagan was good, what made him great were the people he gathered around him—his inner circle. How many cabinet members names do you remember from the various presidents over the past several years—and how many do you remember from the Reagan presidency?" Together we thought of names like George Bush, Alexander Haig, George Shultz, James Baker, Casper Weinberger, Malcolm Baldridge, Elizabeth Dole— names that are very recognizable not only because of serving in Reagan's cabinet but for other important areas of service and contribution for each of them.

Ronald Reagan had leadership strengths, but without his inner circle he could not have accomplished much of anything. He understood this (as all truly great leaders do) and he obviously worked at pulling together the strongest team he could find. And then he took one more very important step—he listened to them.

Abraham Lincoln is thought by many to be the best U.S. president ever. He did much the same as Ronald Reagan; he picked a cabinet that would bring to the presidency the best thought leaders for various situations. They were later labeled a "team of rivals" because some at least had designs on the presidency themselves and Lincoln reasoned that they, therefore, could provide him with the best help in leading the country. It wasn't particularly harmonious, and it could be argued that he might have done better with less contentious people, but the result was that the country was preserved and that continues to this day.

Of course the greatest inner circle story is Jesus and the twelve disciples. He handpicked them, spent three intense years with them coaching, training, being an example, and then He got out of the way. They floundered some but the lessons He taught stuck and have been taught down through the generations to this day—2,000 years later.

Next to having a leader's heart and the character traits to lead, the most important thing for an aspiring leader to have is a team (an inner circle) that supports him or her. So many try to do it on their own, they tolerate the people around them, they try to influence them, but they do not take them into their confidence and share life with them—the good and the bad—and create a sense of we're in this together and together we will succeed!

In chapter 14 we looked at the aspects of leadership and the various styles of leadership and how they support yet are different from each other. It does seem as if some leaders could have all the aspects—it is possible but not likely. Even if a fully-equipped leader did exist, the organization would be better off with more leaders sharing the leadership load. First of all, one leader would likely have a bias toward one aspect and therein not achieve the balance needed. Another reason for including more leaders is to be prepared when the leader moves on. The organization needs to have an experienced replacement who will be ready to succeed the departing leader. Not to mention, leaders need to know when they look for support, they will find it in the inner circle. All of these elements lead to a good overall question, "Why a team?"

A leadership team has been described as, "a complementary team where people's strengths are made productive and their weaknesses made irrelevant by the strengths of others." The result of this is synergism: the whole is greater than the sum of the parts. I used to think that this kind of thinking was just an academic idea, and not particularly practical, until I observed it in action.

I saw it working a little, here and there at first. But then something happened to a team where I served as leader that kicked the reality of a team's importance into high gear. The team consisted of ten white males responsible for a large manufacturing operation. I thought it was a pretty good team relative to other teams I had managed or been a part of. Three things happened that changed the team forever. First, an African American joined the team (he replaced one of the white males); second, a woman replaced another white male; and third, a white male with absolutely no manufacturing experience replaced the current HR manager. A third of the team turned over and with very different new players.

It was bad—we had lost our ability to think fast and get moving. We had to explain things to the newbies that previously we never had to think about. Starting over at the starting line seemed further back than the first time and it seemed like we were making no progress at all.

This went on for several weeks, I was miserable and wondered why I had let it happen. I should have thrown a body block in front of the change and kept it from ever happening. At least, I should have pushed for only one at a time, but I had thought that our team was so good we would quickly absorb the change. I guess I thought our culture would assimilate the new people quickly—they would see how efficient we were and join in to our productivity. I did not anticipate they would have criticisms of what we were doing, or suggest such different ideas from our norm.

Then an interesting thing happened. Some of our debates turned into really different ideas for us to try, and we anticipated new outcomes. We implemented a couple of ideas, and they really worked—they worked well! We tried more and they worked too. Our excitement grew with each success. We gained new ground and it was reflected on our bottom line.

Finally, I noticed that we were working much better together. In fact we were as efficient as we had been before these three newbies joined us, but with much more creativity. Not only were we efficient, we had become effective, we had become innovative—and our bottom line continued to improve. In a word we had become a leadership team like the definition - we had become synergistic—*very* synergistic.

That wasn't all. We came to trust each other and knew we could count on each other. We could speak openly, say what was on our heart, and not be rejected by the others—just the opposite in fact. We each wanted to hear what the others had to say, positive feedback as well as critical comment—all of it. We agreed on an objective because we realized we were all in this together. Enroute to that objective we may disagree about how something should be done, but we worked toward consensus because of our agreement on the objective.

I had been a part of many teams prior to this, and believed in them as an organizational concept. I think, however, this was the beginning for me to see the value of teams as an inner circle, a trusted circle of colleagues wherein even more can be accomplished as leaders. Not only the decision-making and direction-setting kinds of plans, but also the development of each leader. This was the incubator for that to happen.

So the question, "Why a team?" Three reasons:

1. It is the <u>balancing mechanism</u> if allowed to be. It can be every time but the senior leader (the boss) must not only allow it to function as openly as possible, he/she must "role model" what that looks like by being open too. They do this by seeking first to understand, by asking good questions, by being transparent in terms of sharing their heart, dreams, concerns, and by being vulnerable in terms of allowing others to do likewise even if it means hearing some things that are critical toward them.

2. It is the <u>leader development incubator</u>. As the elements above emerge, the team becomes a place for leaders to test ideas, and concepts both in terms of what they are trying to accomplish and in terms of the style in which they are doing it. A team that has "giving and receiving feedback" as part of its culture assures that growing leaders hear the things they need to hear to add to their personal development efforts.

3. This leadership team is <u>the role model</u> for the organization. The culture of the organization will reflect the culture of the senior leader's inner circle—the leadership team. This is not something that only happens over a long period of time. When a leadership team is committed to the kinds of heart and character features

mentioned earlier, and when they have a good balance regarding the aspects of leadership, the organization will respond quickly, parallel to the development of this team.

Characteristics of the Inner Circle

In Chapter 15, *The Heart and Character of a Leader*, we listed several bullet point comments to illustrate what collaboration looks like. They are repeated here in the context of an inner circle:

- It's the people around us—mentors and coaches, peers, followers.
- People who are interested in us and willing to listen to us; who give us feedback and provide fresh perspectives and ideas.
- People who fill the gaps (no leader has it all). Ones who cover us in our weak areas.
- A safe place—a place to talk out dreams and share frustrations.
- A way to share your vision and find encouragement to go for it—at times to hear cautions to which you've been blinded.
- The team that you not only share the vision with, but also the *journey* to achieve it.

Leadership characteristics necessary to achieve a supportive team/inner circle:

Some leaders are much better in achieving a team kind of approach to their personal leadership style than others. What are the characteristics of the ones that do so well?

1. **The leader's belief** that collaboration, a team's collective ability, is greater than the sum of their individual abilities. A supporting belief is theory Y—people want to do well, they want to contribute to something

important and be recognized for it. The leader that is guided by this belief will tend to naturally do the right things in terms of engaging others for the team he/she is responsible.

2. **The leader serves the team**, as opposed to "running" the team. Essentially, it's doing whatever will help each individual develop to their maximum potential and then doing whatever facilitates the members to interact effectively and efficiently as a team—a smooth and seamless unit.

   In doing this the leader claims no credit nor allows the limelight to shine on him/her. It's about the team and doing the best that the team can possibly do—the wins will take care of themselves—to paraphrase John Wooden, the great UCLA basketball coach of the 1970's.

   To repeat a concept from the book *Good to Great* by Jim Collins, he describes a leader of a great company as one you are probably not even aware of, because he or she spends all of their time and energy raising up other leaders. It's as if they have sacrificed themselves for the overall betterment of the enterprise.

3. **The leader's willingness to be transparent as a member of the team.** The leader recognizes he is yoked to the same wagon as all the other members and his/her future success can be attained only with the support of the team. Because of this the leader openly shares hopes and dreams, frustrations and issues and allows the team to know and understand who they are (the leader) and what they are trying to accomplish; so they can truly be supported.

   All of us are attracted to those who genuinely seek our help. When was the last time you said "no" to someone who earnestly and genuinely asked you for help? If the leader is sincere in wanting help from members of the team, the team will (most likely), not only provide it, they will provide it with a sense of zeal and appreciation for being asked.

The key word is sincere. If a leader seeks help as a way to manipulate, the team picks up on it pretty quickly and then the leader has a huge trust issue on his hands. But if it is done genuinely and sincerely, it is actually viewed so positively by the members of the team that they tend to become very loyal to the leader. It's amazing how few leaders do this. The prevalent attitude is, "I don't want to let them see me sweat" or "I don't want to look weak." The reality however, is that being real (being transparent) is the very thing that causes leaders to be strong in the eyes of those who follow them. It produces the humility associated with many great leaders, and it deserves our attention as we think about our own development as leaders.

Results of Transparency

The story of the entrepreneur in Chapter 15 is an excellent illustration of the importance of a team. When he started he had no team but as soon as the business could afford a second person he brought in an individual who shared his values but was very different in terms of skills and abilities. The entrepreneur, to his credit, did not view this addition as an employee—rather a partner and team member, they were now a business with a team of two.

After a few more years and some significant growth both in terms of revenue and people the entrepreneur began to feel a need for a larger team to share the strategic thinking and decision-making efforts of the growing company: product extensions, new offices, development of people and the like.

In determining who should be on this team he did an interesting thing—he based it on who could best join him in thinking together—as opposed to the more typical way of determining the best individuals to represent their area. This may at first sound like a minor difference but it is actually quite significant. The representative approach often winds up as the top individuals of the various business units or functional groups and as such, they are primarily interested in protecting their turf as opposed to the company overall.

The approach used by this entrepreneur resulted in a team of very different individuals bringing different points of views all aimed at figuring out what is best for the business—not what is best for their particular area of responsibility. The result is much more commitment to the total success of the business.

There is a second important ingredient for this very successful team. The entrepreneur leader is very transparent both in terms of who he is and in what he is thinking. His process for making a decision is to put all of his thoughts on the table and expect all members of the team to do likewise. From here the debate and discussion begins and continues until consensus is reached. It is rare for the team to not come to a consensus eventually, and if this happens the leader takes the responsibility to make the decision as he should. For the most part, however, they do reach an agreement and the commitment to actualizing the determination is unanimous.

Additionally, the entrepreneur is equally transparent regarding his own personal journey: his dreams, his shortcomings, aspects he would like to improve in and so forth. This encourages the other members of the team to do likewise, which leads to tremendous support—one for the other—along with a noticeable lack of personal ego issues.

One other characteristic that one would notice, if they were to observe this team in action, is that the entrepreneur leader is not boss-like! In fact, it would be difficult to tell just who the boss is. No one is boss-like, but each one takes

the initiative to lead out when it is appropriate to do so—
typically when the subject at hand is something they have a
particular expertise for.

The result of all this, as one would expect, is exceptional
success in what they are doing. Not perfection, but a very
high batting average.

Building Consensus

In the above illustration the team of the entrepreneur
leader would debate and discuss until a consensus was
reached. Logically, for a team to be most effective the members must agree on the objective and how to achieve it for
any opportunity or issue that they are faced with. However,
the reality of all team members actually agreeing on anything is remote, different people have different ideas and
opinions. Actually, those differences are like multiple inputs
that produce a bigger "synergistic" result than if only one
person's input is involved. However if the differences can't
be molded into a common approach, they can be harmful to
the team dynamic to the point of failure. In fact, a continuing
failure to resolve differences can lead to the "boss" determining to make all of the decisions – maybe after gathering
input from all concerned, but often independent of that. "It's
faster and just as effective" he/she would say.

Faster yes but probably not as effective; what happens
when a boss makes all the decisions? Eventually the members of his/her team become less committed to finding the
best way to go, and ultimately they are not committed to the
resulting process at all. They are compliant (doing what the
boss wants - after all they need the paycheck), but they feel
no commitment or passion to do things well.

So what is the solution, how does a team go about finding
the agreement needed? We really don't want a boss to decide
everything and we know that we'll never just agree. These
two things are like the opposite end of a spectrum:

Agree   Boss decide

Is there something in the middle? What if, instead a single boss deciding, we thought of each team member as a "situational leader" – having expertise in some areas. We could assign a decision that needs to be made to the one most qualified to handle it. Perhaps the team would give some input to this individual as they take it on, but then they would do whatever is needed to understand it, and make the decisions necessary to move forward on it.

Or, perhaps a "sub team" of two or three could take responsibility to learn what needs to be understood and then prepare a recommendation to bring back to the team for the final decision. The team may make some refinement suggestions that the sub team would incorporate and then the team could "sign off"; ie, approve the recommended action.

Or, a third approach could be for the team to "build consensus" regarding a decision that needs to be made. Consensus means to work to agreement*. The members of the team put their individual ideas on the table and then discuss and debate the relative merits of each. They look for common ground, "give and take" regarding their own ideas and opinions, until an agreement is forged. (*Consensus decision making is a group decision making process that seeks the consent, not necessarily the agreement of participants, and the resolution of objectives. Wikipedia)

In order for this to work a few rules need to be established:

   1. Debate and discussion is vital and everyone must participate

2. "Give and take" will be necessary (members can't hold on to their opinion at the expense of the team finding the decision to be made)
3. If consensus can't be reached then the team leader will decide (this could be a "situational leader" determined in advance to take that responsibility if needed).

So now we have a decision making spectrum with more options – and we can stay away from the extremes:

Agree	*Consensus*	*Recommendation*	*Situational Leader*	Boss decide

The reality for most teams is that very few decisions need to be worked to consensus by the whole team working together – most can be handled by assigning items to "situational leaders" with input from the team. A few bigger decisions can be handled by a sub team developing a recommendation. Only a few items that have very large impact would go through the team discussion/give and take process indicated. With these the team would be wise to set up a time boundary before beginning: ie, how much time will we work this before turning it over to the leader that will step in and decide if no consensus is reached. (By the way once a team gets used to the process this rarely happens because the team members self monitor themselves in a way that gets the job done before hand – no one likes to admit defeat).

The other point that needs to be made is that all of the possibilities mentioned above are consensus building. Whether the team agrees to have one of their members take an item and work it, or assign it to a sub team to work up a recommendation, or work it though to an agreement, it is all consensus - the team is <u>agreeing</u> on how to handle the work they have to do. As they have learned how to do this they have developed themselves as a synergistic team – they have become adept in taking all of the ideas of each member and finding a common approach to move forward. Also, this can be transferred to other teams in an organization with an ultimate result of becoming a consensus building culture.

Creating the Culture

The development of the entrepreneur's inner circle, along with strong beliefs regarding what the culture of his young company should be, were foundational to what has become a very successful company.

He knew what he didn't want regarding culture because of what he experienced when he worked for the first company. He had never worked in a company that had the culture he desired but he had some ideas. For example, he wanted: 1) to hire people who were selfless team players, 2) a culture that was totally honest—that would never cut a corner; 3) a culture that was technically excellent and treated customers with the highest degree of excellence, etc. He didn't have these written down, he just knew what he wanted it to look like and he ensured that the first person he recruited desired these same objectives.

That was the beginning. Two quickly grew to several, and they determined that each new team member would embrace these cultural ideas. Today, there are hundreds, and those original leaders continue to assure that everyone embraces their cultural ideals. To do this they have developed techniques and approaches to assure that everyone understands what the principles and expected behavior are for the culture of the company. Even though the company is growing larger they refuse to compromise those original ideals.

Some leaders would say, "Why bother? I just want a lean, mean machine as an organizational culture. If I have that the rest will work out just fine." The truth is, you can't force efficiency, but you can have it if the people in the organization are committed to it. If you force it you may get compliance, but you won't see that extra effort that only comes with a culture that encourages everyone to participate and be committed.

Who is affected most by your organization's culture? Your customers. That's where the rubber meets the road. The reputation an enterprise develops is directly related to its culture, and it's that reputation that grows the company.

What Makes a Culture?

Culture is defined as: *the set of shared attitudes, values, goals, and practices that characterizes an institution or organization* (Webster). Examples might be a corporate culture focused on the bottom line or an enterprise focused on a set of multiple bottom lines such as the wellbeing of the employees and the community in which you operate, along with the typical financial bottom line.

What do we want our culture to look like and how do we want it to function? What shared practices will characterize our culture? We may not have thought a lot about this but if do, we all know some aspects we would want in a workplace.

Whenever people gather together and stay together for a common cause or objective, a culture will emerge—however, what that culture looks like is anybody's guess. If there are leaders it may resemble what the leaders believe but often the leaders believe different things and behave differently themselves. This leaves the emerging organization to sort of find its own way. Some organizations are a collection of mini cultures or cliques. Others have some general negative tendencies because of the way they are led. We have all experienced interaction with a business that is not particularly friendly or helpful—a reflection of its leadership.

On the other hand we have also experienced organizations that just can't seem to do enough for you, and you look forward to the next opportunity with them. As you think of such a company you wonder what their work culture is like and you think, "That is probably a great place to work."

What is it about those kinds of work culture that catches our attention? How would you describe it? Here are some ideas from my own observations:

Clearly Understood Core Values

Deciding on and stating an organization's core values is the responsibility of the primary, "senior" leader and his leadership team—his inner circle. They must do two things:

First, they must assure that there is a set of core values upon which all leaders agree. These must be developed by the leadership team, but can be "informed" by asking for input from the entire organization. This can provide broad organizational understanding and ownership from the beginning. As the organization grows the core values can be re-examined as a technique of keeping the organization connected.

One technique to develop core values is for each leader to individually write down their own core values and then compare notes. Where there is agreement is a good place to start the discussion—common ground. Input from the organization can be added in at this point as well.

The method above should provide a starting point of five to ten core values. From there it is a matter of debate and discussion to arrive at a consensus in order to build the organizational culture.

Second, the leaders must role model and propagate these values. This means walking the talk and actions that facilitate understanding by the organization; such as teaching and facilitating discussions that explain the "why" behind the core value as well as the "how to."

Selfless Servers

True leaders understand that the route to greatness is a willingness to start at the bottom, and learn and grow from there. As part of this, they are always willing to help another person even if it requires sacrifice. This attitude, repeated across the organization, is powerful. It is the beginning attitude that launches all the rest, like teamwork, innovation, customer service and just plain excellence in everything that is done.

Our society seems to have a lot of "me first" thinkers. They can be highly talented but they have an attitude of taking care of themselves first. We even have an acronym for it WIIFM—"What's in it for me?" This attitude is in opposition to creating a great work culture.

Behavior Matches Core Values

Being consistent is obvious but not always easy. It starts with recruiting people who have the cultural characteristics you want in your culture. Done well this can accomplish half of what will be needed right from the start, but, it will not complete all of it. The rest will come from the leaders, and eventually others in the organization, walking the talk and propagating the core values of the organization.

What are the behaviors we might see in a successful culture?

People who:
- Are direct and truthful in all interactions
- Always meet commitments
- Start relationships in the trust mode
- Are open to hearing and sharing information
- Are widely trusted
- Are learning and growing
- Are seeking to improve the processes they work on

And an organization that consistently demonstrates:
- Friendliness
- Desire to serve

- Effective teamwork: seamless interaction in the transfer of information and duties between members
- Innovation and flexibility: able and willing to think outside of the box to work toward different accomplishments
- Willingness to change: they understand and embrace the need for change to keep up in the global marketplace.
- Technical excellence, for the products and/or services they provide

There are many ways to describe a work culture, the important thing the leaders of an organization must do is first determine what they want their culture to look like. What are the characteristics and behaviors that you want? Answer that—then set about to develop it.

Leadership that builds effective organizational culture

In Summary, leadership begins with the heart and character of the individual leader. As the leader builds his or her team—the inner circle—this heart and character is transferred to the team; not automatically but through a process of discussion and agreeing on what the important principles are. This leadership team is hugely important:

- It is the balancing mechanism that facilitates the strengths of each member and makes each member's weakness irrelevant through the strengths of the others. The result is synergism—the whole is greater than the sum of the parts.
- It is the leader development incubator—a safe place to test ideas, give and receive feedback, and be encouraged to take on new initiatives.
- It is the role model for the organization. The culture of the organization is a reflection of the leadership team.

When this team is committed to the kinds of heart and character traits described earlier and when they are aligned and working together, the organization will respond, parallel to the development of this team.

How do you do all of this? It begins when the leadership team regularly interacts with each other, processes the core values they collectively believe in, develops a vision for the future, and designs an approach to share all of this with the organization they are leading.

As these elements become understood by everyone involved (the organization at large) it is time to develop a plan of action to achieve it all—and for this the participation of everyone in the organization is crucial. A variety of approaches can be used such as representative teams to develop portions of the plan, work projects, and solve problems. Also, a consistent communications approach must be developed that connects each individual, each team and the organization overall. The objective of this communications approach is simply that none are left out of the loop and that no one is ever surprised with news of something that affects them but they didn't see coming. More on this topic in the next chapter.

All other details can be developed in ways that fit with the organizational character that exists—but the points mentioned here will serve well as a beginning framework. Combine the capability of the leader and his/her team to establish the overall direction and core values mentioned, and the organization will achieve the desired culture.

Chapter 18

The Role of Communications

O ver many years of observing leaders in a variety of situations I have concluded that most believe that communication is about talking. After all, they might say, how else can I lead if I don't let people know the direction I want to lead them? Of course, there is some truth to that. However, for many leaders, communication stops where it should be just beginning.

Typical leaders are, by nature, strong individuals, and they have learned how to make things happen through excelling at explaining and clarifying what they think needs to be done. In the process they forget an important reality— the people they are trying to lead have a brain and a heart and likely some pretty good ideas about how to go forward themselves. Leaders who don't pay attention to this lose the opportunity to gain the commitment of those they're trying to lead. Oh, they may get them to follow, compliantly (especially if they are being paid, less if not), but they will never gain their commitment. Isn't commitment a better outcome than compliance?

In order to gain commitment we must tap into the hearts and minds of those we are trying to lead. We must seek a more collaborative approach and be willing to share the power—the power of ideas and involvement in decisions regarding things that affect the team. The leader that masters this will become that Level 5 leader Jim Collins speaks of in his book *Good to Great*. A Level 5 leader facilitates direction by raising up other leaders, rather than being the sole source of direction.

The universal skill required by all leaders is the skill of communication, 1) to listen and understand, 2) to effectively role model the desired behaviors expected of everyone, and 3) the capability to present information, ideas, and vision in a way that is clear and understandable.

Listening

One of Stephen Covey's *Seven Habits of Highly Effective People* is to, "Seek first to understand, then to be understood." The old saying, "We have two ears and one tongue, so we should listen twice as much as talk" is pretty good advice. Listening and understanding should be the first arrow in our communication quiver and we're wise to be very slow moving beyond this until we thoroughly understand it.

This is easy to say but hard to do. I'm not aware of any leader that finds this easy. It just seems to go against the grain of a leader's makeup, which is typically to move forward and get things done. It is hard to really listen when you think you know what to do—you're ready to get on with it. But, disciplining yourself to do this (and do it well), is paramount to having your most important asset—the people in your organization—go with you.

Role Modeling

People determine a lot about leaders based on how well their actions match their messages. Our behavior and body language says much about us and indicates the degree to which we can be trusted as authentic. We damage this repu-

220

tation when we show our minds are elsewhere. Physical signals say a lot, such as: rolling our eyes, looking at our watches (or smart phones), looking away from the one talking to us to watch what others are doing…we pretend we're listening to someone explain or complain but our actions show our minds are elsewhere. The message is pretty clear, "I'm really not interested in you or what you are saying." We've just discredited any sort of valuable communication.

Contrast that with a person who looks you in the eye as if you are the only person in the world, gives no indication of being in a hurry, smiles, nods their head and generally gives off body language that you really matter and what you are saying is as important to them as it is to you. They offer the occasional question to show they comprehend the importance of the conversation, which engages you even more and draws out the finer nuances of the matter. You'll find yourself opening up like talking to an old friend.

Presenting

Doing the first two aspects are key to others wanting to hear what you have to say. It unlocks the door or filters to an individual's hearing. But the presenting part must be done in a way that is respectful, conversational, not long-winded or preachy and seasoned with questions to draw the other into a conversation that becomes a dialogue—as opposed to "now it's my turn to tell you what I think."

Out of this respectful dialogue a multitude of wonderful outcomes occur: issues solved, direction determined, a relationship formed, a basis established for future conversation, maybe even a friendship begun.

Presenting in a group context is enhanced by the presenter first being a very good listener and role model. The role model part is especially important. Crowds will form to hear presentations from leaders who have set an outstanding example. But, even in our everyday lives, our ability to be heard starts with who we are and the examples we portray in daily life.

Some presentation principles:
- Keep the presentation focused and brief.
- Use good examples and illustrations to enhance understanding.
- Avoid "I"—both the word and the context (too many illustrations about "me" loses listeners).
- Allow for group interaction: a simple exercise that provides a way for the audience to give input/ideas, ask questions, etc.
- Consolidate the information received with the information you are presenting as a summary for the communications effort (provide something that can cause everyone to feel like they had involvement and some say in the process).
- All of this must be done in a way that is always respectful and empathetic—resulting in the recipient(s) feeling valued and cared for.

There is nothing a leader does in terms of leading, that doesn't require some element of this communication skill set. There are three contexts in which communication occurs: 1) a one-to-one individual interaction, 2) a small group meeting, or 3) a large group interaction. Each has a different dynamic and requires somewhat different aspects from your communication skill set.

One-to-One Discussion

When I began my career I was the team manager for 14 technicians making Pampers disposable diapers. I was encouraged to have regular one-to-one coaching discussions with each of these technicians on a regular basis—every two weeks. This did not take the place of the daily interactions a leader has with each person he is responsible for, rather it was a time to sit down together, away from the workplace, and talk about how things were going for the individual. The discussion could focus on training, performance, career development, or any number of specific questions or issues the individual might have. It was the foundational element of the communication skill set and therefore, the foundation of our coaching. Today, 40 years later, these principles continue to be a good guide:

- Always work toward building and maintaining relationships.
- "Seek first to understand, then to be understood."
- Value each person:
  - o Each is different but important
  - o Let them maintain dignity and self-esteem
  - o Acknowledge the right to his/her perception
  - o Help them make free and informed choices
- Take steps toward improvement of the situation.
- Summarize key points and action steps.
- Make the one-to-one a regular interaction.
- Three questions for one-to-one "check-ups":
  - o How is it going?
  - o What are you trying to achieve?
  - o How can I help?

The emphasis should always be to hear, understand and help individuals find their way in terms of direction, improvement, new opportunities, resolving issues etc. This gives the person being communicated to a greater sense of ownership and commitment to the outcome of the discussion.

Feedback
Feedback is needed for an individual to develop and it should be a part of the one-to-one discussion. It is done as

part of a normal conversation that occurs on a regular basis. Because of this, the feedback feels more organic and is appreciated by the recipient. If the individual is not accustomed to regular interaction, the feedback will be unexpected and often unwelcome. It can be as simple as, "Here is my observation..." and then describe whatever it is that you want the person to know from your perspective. Note: feedback is both positive (validating) and/or constructive (improvement needed).

Some tips regarding feedback:
- Tell the person what you observed clearly and accurately (don't beat around the bush).
- When giving feedback, provide examples.
- Share your own experience with the situation/example being discussed.
- Always invite the person to respond, add to, and take the first step in what would be the appropriate action step for the constructive (improvement needed) feedback.
- Establish a follow-up step for the action plan, to reconnect and review progress as needed (again, as much as possible, let the person receiving the feedback take the initiative as to when and how this will occur. If there is a regular scheduled one-to-one meeting anyway, this will be the likely forum).
- Note: Be a good role model yourself in receiving feedback. Don't be defensive, ask questions to understand, and indicate appreciation for the feedback.

Resolving Conflict
There are times when the emotional and frustration level is high and it isn't possible to follow the suggested course of action—this leads to conflict with others. More direction from the leader is necessary to resolve discord and differences. Some principles for handling disputes:

- Deal face to face with the individuals involved in the conflict. Always be respectful. Do not let your own emotions rise and cause you to be argumentative, speak more loudly than normal or be disrespectful in any way.
- Acknowledge the conflict (get it on the table) with all involved.
- Separate the emotion tied to the situation from problem-solving*.
- Identify the source of the conflict:
  o Understand each point of view.
  o Separate symptoms from the root cause — the source.
  o Realize, often the perceived problem is not the actual problem.
  o Work until agreement is reached regarding the source.
- Establish a plan to deal with the source of the conflict.
- Follow up with all key people involved to assure the plan is being implemented or appropriately adjusted.

*Separating emotion from problem-solving is extremely important. There is no value in trying to move forward until this is done. The ability to think and/or act rationally is impaired by the emotion. To separate it the leader must first avoid engaging in it and maintain a level-headed, rational, and patient posture. If, in the course of discussion, the emotions remain high then it is probably necessary to suspend the discussion until the emotional person(s) settles down and is able to think and interact rationally.

This cooling off period could take a few minutes or it could take several hours. The only way to know for sure is to: 1) stop the discussion, 2) separate the individuals involved (make sure this is done in a way where no injury can occur to themselves or to others), 3) keep an eye on the individuals and check occasionally with brief interaction so you can evaluate how they are doing. When, in your judgment, the individuals involved are cooled down, resume the discussion.

If the situation is particularly charged emotionally, it may be wise to involve others in assessing this step and it may also be wise to literally let the individuals sleep on it, by not reconvening the discussion until the next day.

The Small Group

In addition to coaching each technician one-to-one, I also was responsible to develop the fourteen into a team. This required a different communications dynamic. In our case we had a 30-minute meeting prior to each shift to discuss the results of the previous shifts and prepare for our upcoming shift. As my responsibilities increased, the focus of what became a leadership team changed, but the need for effective small group meetings continued. The following provides guidance for small group communications:

- All of the principles and concepts described for one-to-one communications apply. Of course some things, like giving feedback, change a bit in a group setting. For example, you would not give individual feedback, especially a personal issue that needs correction in the presence of the entire group. You would only do that in a one-to-one setting.
- Additional preparation becomes necessary with a group:
    - o Knowing when to convene the group (and when not to).
    - o What sort of meeting will it be? (Decision making, consensus building, gathering input, determining subcommittees; information sharing; training, etc).

o Meeting logistics (room setup, etc).
o Agenda
o Pre-work if appropriate (with good instructions).
o Start and end on time.
o Clarity regarding next steps.
- Understanding how to lead decision-making discussions (Building Consensus – Chapter 17).
- Establish an effective process to follow up and evaluate progress regarding team next steps plan.

Large Groups

Large groups could be described as any group larger than 10 to 12 individuals. A small group is necessary for dialogue and debate. As the group size increases this becomes more and more difficult to do, to the point of interaction being virtually impossible.

The best communication for a large group is information sharing, and it is common in organizations for the key leader or leaders to do this as a kind of "state of the business" presentation. This is scheduled with regular frequency—typically monthly or quarterly. Leaders have also had success combining information sharing with receiving input from the group by facilitating small group discussions around a certain question(s) after the information sharing is complete. The information from these small group discussions is compiled for use in developing a next steps plan.

Some principles and concepts for large group communication:
- Follow all of the principles and concepts outlined with small groups, with the exception of attempting anything along the line of consensus decision making or individual feedback.
- The amount of time spent sharing information should be reasonably short—typically 20 minutes or less. It should be an elaboration of material available to read

(either in printed form or via projection on a screen/video monitor, etc.).

- Be clear in what you expect the recipients to do with the information you are sharing.
- Allow time for a questions-and-answers (Q & A) segment.
- Provide a short summary of the meeting and dismiss the group on time.
- In some cases it is appropriate to follow up the meeting with a written summary to all participants.

The large group meeting can be a precursor to one-to-one discussions and/or small group meetings. For example, the large group meeting serves as a "kick off" to more in-depth discussions that follow in small groups or on a one-to-one basis. It launches the big picture, and leaves room for specifics to be discussed in smaller settings.

Summarizing Communication

Communication is a very broad, multi-faceted subject. The principles and concepts shared here provide a good foundation from which to start. These provide important building blocks for everything a leader does: setting direction, communicating core values, developing more leaders, developing teams and organizational effectiveness, etc. Effective communications act as a connector for everything an organization needs; done well it creates a kind of organizational "glue" that sets up the potential for great things to occur.

Afterword

The Rest of the Story

My objective in telling the *Back to the Cottage* story was to present the importance of certain values necessary in the workplace to achieve real success—success fueled by the enthusiasm and commitment of each person involved. I did not intend for it to be biographical or some sort of testimony to my own performance through the years. However, to accomplish my objective I did need to tell my story to a degree. The combination of my family's cottage industry and my evolving role working with companies throughout my career contributed to my point of view on this subject of workplace values. There is more I would like to explain regarding my personal journey.

As I described in an earlier chapter, growing up was a pretty ideal time for me—small town, farm, good parents, sports, etc. I don't ever remember feeling like I was someone special nor did I feel insignificant. I was just a kid growing up. Then I went to college. I was the first in my family to do so and though it was a small college, I thought it was huge. As a decent football and baseball player, I wound up playing both sports in college. Halfway through the baseball season that first spring I led the conference in hitting. I think that might have been the first time I thought I was something special.

The following year I played starting defensive back on the football team and by my senior year I was co-captain and quarterback—the position I also played in high school. My grades were decent and I had been elected to be one of our class officers. It is no wonder that I needed a size 7½ helmet—my head had swollen significantly.

I didn't realize what was happening to me of course, but now as I look at my picture in the college yearbook I can see attitude written all over my face. That picture was taken at the beginning of the season. At the halfway mark we were terrible. We had lost most of our games, morale was low and our new coach made lots of mistakes—at least it seemed that way to me. I determined to do something about it—I decided to have a talk with him.

As it turned out the dismalness of our season paled in contrast with the dismalness of my performance with the coach. I must have handled it really poorly because the next day my locker was cleaned out—his way of saying, "you're fired!" I was released without anything in the way of explanation (although I heard later that the coach had characterized me as having a "superior attitude"). Clearly, I had failed in accomplishing my intentions, but not clear in how or why I had failed. At that point I didn't consider fighting back—I just left the team.

Earlier in the book, I described starting with Procter and Gamble after completing college and how I had another leadership failure. A technician on my team was injured in a small work accident and, as manager, I was to provide a brief accident report in the monthly safety meeting—attended by many of the top leaders in the organization. As I began the presentation I froze up and had to be bailed out by my boss. The brash young man of twenty who had the moxie (if not the technique) to talk to the head coach about his performance was now afraid to stand up and speak for himself.

But this time the coach hung in there with me as I worked through the problem and overcame my speaking shyness. In the process I learned a valuable principle that was outside the corporate norms of that time—the value of valuing people—which began a quest to learn more that continues to this day.

This coach's intervention in my life was hugely significant – professionally! But it didn't solve the problems I was having at home.

Flashback to my college days again. The growth of the "big head" was accompanied by a growing fondness for alcohol. Thank God, there weren't any drugs readily available or who knows what my lifestyle would have included. Also, I was not unaware of the attractive members of the opposite sex, I liked what I saw, but when conversation started the attractiveness dimmed.

Then I met Kathie! Kathie was extremely attractive, beautiful really; yet she was different. She was not focused on herself like so many attractive, young women tend to be. I found myself talking with her for hours on end—and I fell in love. We married and over the next several years began raising our daughters—three of them. Sounds fine, right? Well, it could have been except for the fact that I was a lousy husband and father. See, I had gotten past my professional difficulties and I was doing pretty well again. The big head returned, along with the alcohol—oh, and did I mention cigarettes? A pack and a half a day. I was dependable at work, and undependable at home. My daughters didn't know whether I would be sweet or a grouch. I left the childrearing to Kathie and got involved only when I was mad about something they had done. As a result they became brats. It's no wonder, based on what their father role-modeled.

Then another significant, life-changing event. I became a believer in Jesus Christ. It was a progressive change—a combination of beginning to realize what a self-centered slob I was, some new friends (also believers), and a loving wife who didn't give up on me. Shortly after I made that important life decision the miracle happened. My children stopped being brats and became truly well behaved, loving daughters (they were already beautiful).

This is how it happened. Deloris and Richard Stalvey became our friends. They were about our age but miles ahead of us in the quality of their marriage. We began getting together and spent hours draining them of everything they understood about being married and raising children. I learned about unconditional love, what being "one with your wife" really means, and how to be a father to my children. They taught me how to praise and encourage my children and the right way to discipline them—and do it in a consistent loving way that doesn't exasperate (Ephesians 6:4).

It wasn't long before I decided to give it a try, to put into action the ideas Deloris and Richard taught us. In two weeks the miracle happened. My daughters were happy, well adjusted, normal little girls and I was their happy camper father. From that point on I was interested to know the biblical principle for other issues. At one point I described to another new friend the values we incorporated in the workplace—cottage values as I later came to think of them. As I described them he said, "Sounds very biblical!" I had never thought of a workplace being biblical—but I decided to check it out. Here is what I found:

The Value of Knowing What You Stand For
- We are God's children—heirs of God and co-heirs with Christ (Romans 8:17)
- We are God's workmanship; created to do good works (Ephesians 2:10)
- As for me and my household, we will follow the Lord (Joshua 24:15)

The Value of Knowing Where You are Going
- Without a vision, the people cast off restraint—they perish (Proverbs 29:18)
- Be careful how you live, not as unwise but as wise, making the most of every opportunity (Ephesians 5:15-16)

The Value of Honest and Integrity
- Let your yes be yes and your no, no (Matthew 5:37)
- The man of integrity walks securely (Proverbs 10:9)

The Value of Planning
- Commit to the Lord whatever you do, and your plans will succeed (Proverbs 16:3)
- The plans of the diligent lead to profit (Proverbs 21:5)

The Value of Each Individual
- Before I formed you in the womb, I knew you (Jeremiah 1:5)
- I am fearfully and wonderfully made (Psalms 139:14)

The Value of Teamwork
- Two are better than one—they have a good return for their work (Ecclesiastes 4:9)
- One body, many parts (1 Corinthians 12:12-26)

The Value of Continual Learning and Development
- Let the wise listen and add to their learning (Proverbs 1:5)
- By wisdom is a house built, through understanding it is established, through knowledge its rooms are filled with rare and beautiful treasures (Proverbs 24:3-4)

He was right, our Cottage values did have a biblical basis—or maybe said another way, a Judeo-Christian ethic.

Although I had never thought of it that way, it did make sense. Our country was founded on this code of ethics and certainly much of what we are as a society, though often debated, is based on these same principles.

So what is my point? Am I saying that the only way to lead is to become a follower of Jesus Christ and the principles of the Bible? No, actually these principles are so good that they will work for any organization, provided leaders and teams have the heart to make them a priority. They can't treat it as the program of the day only to be discarded when the going gets tough, or someone comes in at a high leadership level with a better idea.

But, I will also acknowledge that I doubt I would ever have been able to do what I do without this life-changing experience. I shudder to think what might have been had I continued in the egotistical ways of those early adult years. But, by God's grace, "what might have been" never happened. Instead, He intervened and this life shared in this book is the end result. "That's my story and I'm sticking to it" as the song goes.

So I continue on in my journey, amazed most of the time and occasionally frustrated at what life brings my way—but never disappointed in my decision those many years ago to follow the creator and sustainer of my life.

The season of life I now find myself in is proving to be the best ever—not that I have life all figured out. I won't ever know it all, at least in this lifetime—but the journey is terrific. I wouldn't trade these years with any that have gone before and I look forward, with great anticipation, to the years to come. When it comes time to pass on to the next life, I hope it can be said of me that "he looked after his family, was a faithful friend, and passed along a couple of good ideas for the next generation."

John Sipple

About the Author

John Sipple has 35 years experience in manufacturing management with Fortune 50 companies such as Dupont, Procter and Gamble, and International Paper. Sipple is currently president of his own company, The Business Resource Network, which he founded to bring together experienced leaders to help other leaders achieve success in the Global Marketplace.

Sipple received his degree in Mathematics from Marietta College, Ohio, spent two years with Dupont as a project engineer, and then signed on with Procter and Gamble where he spent 27 years. He progressed from first level supervision in Procter's new paper division (Pampers, Bounty, Charmin) to manufacturing director. During his tenure he managed several of the company's largest facilities in the U.S., Canada, and Europe. In his professional career, John was involved in over 20 successful organizational start-ups or change processes, and is an expert in change management strategies.

During these years Procter and Gamble was developing their version of High Performance Work Systems, a high involvement, team-based approach, which is heavily dependent on an effective "coaching" style of leadership. Sipple was a key contributor to the effort; his areas of responsibility always reflected this cutting edge approach with world-class results. Today, Sipple and others who work with him via The Business Resource Network are involved in similar transformations in a variety of businesses and non-profit organizations. BRN is a management consulting firm that specializes in executive coaching and leadership development.

John and his wife Kathie have three married daughters, and eight grandchildren. They live in Fayetteville, Georgia (Atlanta) and are very active in a number of volunteer activities including The Navigators, for which John serves as associate staff, and several other organizations for which both Kathie and John serve as board members.

CPSIA information can be obtained at www.ICGtesting.com
Printed in the USA
LVOW040828180312

273458LV00001B/5/P